Mr Whatnot

A comedy

Alan Ayckbourn

Samuel French - London
New York - Toronto - Hollywood

ISBN 0 573 11287 8

Please see page iv for further copyright information.

MR WHATNOT

First performed at the Victoria Theatre, Stoke-on-Trent in November 1963, *Mr Whatnot* transferred to the Arts Theatre, London in August 1964. *Mr Whatnot* was later seen at the Stephen Joseph Theatre in the Round in Scarborough in 1976 and was revived at the New Victoria Theatre, Newcastle-under-Lyme in 1988.

CHARACTERS

Mint
Lord Slingsby-Craddock
Lady Slingsby-Craddock, his wife
Amanda, their daughter
Cecil, her fiancé
A Tweedy Lady
A Pedestrian
A Butler
A Maid
A Gardener
A Vicar

The action of the play takes place in and around Craddock Grange

Time—Saturday night and Sunday morning

AUTHOR'S PREFACE

Mr Whatnot is a play for actors who can move and mime—rather than for mime artists. Don't get hung up on the mime, it's only there to make things quicker and more fantastic, never as an end in itself. The play is a tribute to every silent film comedian that ever lived, most especially the great Buster Keaton who understood more than most how deadly serious, how unselfconscious good comedy always is.

Alan Ayckbourn would like to thank James Earls-Davis of the New Victoria Theatre, Newcastle-under-Lyme for his invaluable help with the Effects Plot.

Other plays by Alan Ayckbourn
published by Samuel French Ltd

One Act

A Cut in the Rates
Ernie's Incredible Illucinations

Full Length

Absent Friends
Absurd Person Singular
Bedroom Farce
A Chorus of Disapproval
Confusions
Henceforward . . .
How the Other Half Loves
Intimate Exchanges (volumes 1 and 2)
Joking Apart
Just Between Ourselves
Living Together
Man of the Moment
Mixed Doubles (with other authors)
The Norman Conquests
Relatively Speaking
Season's Greetings
Sisterly Feelings
A Small Family Business
Table Manners
Taking Steps
Ten Times Table
Time and Time Again
Tons of Money (revised)
Way Upstream
Woman in Mind

ACT I

Scene A

Introduction music

Mint enters. He stands for a moment

Voice Over Watch this man closely. He is a piano tuner.

He moves forward fumbling in his pockets for his front door key. He finds it and opens his front door. He closes the door behind him. He is carrying a small black bag which he places on the floor. He goes into the kitchen. He fills the kettle at the sink. He places the kettle on the stove and lights the gas. He sees and hears his cat. He fills a saucer of milk and places it on the floor. The cat purrs. He returns to the sitting-room, switches on the radio, picks up a newspaper and sits down to read it. The radio blares out a noisy foreign programme. He then leans over and dials until he finds some piano music, which appears to please him. After a moment he opens the newspaper and reads. He remains seated as:

The lights fade. Music changes to introduce an elegant drawing-room

Scene B

Lord Slingsby-Craddock enters. Elderly, near-sighted, vague, at times highly irascible. Lady Slingsby-Craddock follows. A charming middle-aged woman. A socialite. With her a Tweedy Lady, hatted, huntin', ominously shaped. Amanda, their daughter, next, a vacant, beautiful, willow-like debutante with a high, thin voice that is almost back projected. Lastly, Cecil, her chinless fiancé. Long straight hair. Long straight public school trained body. They all wear enormous straw sunhats

There is an actual piano stool, but we imagine the piano

Lord Slingsby-Craddock There! (*He indicates the piano with his shooting stick*) Quite a good piano, I believe. Nobody's actually ever played it.
Tweedy Lady What do you play? Rockin' and Rollin', or boogie woogie?
Cecil (*who lisps*) Oh, no well—actually I'm really rather mostly classical really.
Amanda Oh, marvellous.
Cecil Sort of Beethoven—Brahms. Anything beginning with a B, that's me.

They all laugh loudly and metallically

Lady Slingsby-Craddock (*above the laughter*) Quiet everybody!
Amanda Sssh. (*She giggles*)

A pause. Cecil steps forward to the piano. There is long business while he loosens his fingers etc. Cecil sits. Pause. He strikes a chord. Applause from the listeners

Lady Slingsby-Craddock		Superb . . .
Tweedy Lady	(*together*)	Bravo . . . bravo
Amanda		Oh, I say . . . I say—I say . . .

Cecil (*laughing nervously*) Bit rusty.
Lord Slingsby-Craddock Brand new piano . . .
Cecil No . . . me.

They all laugh

Amanda Go on, go on, Cecil—go on . . .
Lady Slingsby-Craddock Sssh . . .
Lord Slingsby-Craddock Sssshhhh.

Silence. Cecil plays the same chord followed by a flurry of notes. He stops suddenly

Cecil Oh, I say . . .
Lord Slingsby-Craddock What the devil's the matter?
Cecil It's flat. Piano's flat. Flat as a pancake.
Amanda Pancake! (*She screams with laughter*) Pancake—flat as a pancake. (*She goes into hysterics*)
Lord Slingsby-Craddock Bally thing can't be flat. Bally thing's brand new. Send the bally thing back if the bally thing's flat.
Cecil Flat. Absolutely flat.
Amanda Flat as a pancake. (*She laughs*)
Lady Slingsby-Craddock Amanda! Control, darling.
Amanda (*contritely*) Sorry, Mummy.
Cecil Piano tuner. That's what it wants.
Lord Slingsby-Craddock Piano tuner? Don't think we've got one.
Cecil Can't play without one. Sorry—dreadfully sorry. Can't play. Just can't play at all. Listen to it . . . (*He strikes a note, at the treble end*)
Lady Slingsby-Craddock Yes, see what you mean. (*She strikes a note, in the middle of the keyboard*)
Lord Slingsby-Craddock Sounds all right to me. (*He strikes a note, bass*)
Amanda Bravo. Bravo. Well played—encore! (*She giggles*)
Cecil Sorry. I must change my flannels. Excuse me. (*He makes to leave*)
Amanda Wait for me, Cecil. (*As they go*) Aren't you going to play, Cecil, I wanted to hear you play.
Cecil I can't play while it's like that. Most dreadfully needs a tuner. It's the only thing—a tuner.

Cecil and Amanda go out

Tweedy Lady Must have a piano tuner.

Lord Slingsby-Craddock grunts

Lady Slingsby-Craddock Telephone—of course, telephone. (*She opens a telephone book*) Taxi ... Taxidermist ... Territorial Army ... Tennis Club ... Ah, Tuner ... Piano Tuner. Maple six-six-five-four-one-two-three. Here you are.
Lord Slingsby-Craddock Eh?
Lady Slingsby-Craddock Phone. It's *your* piano, darlin'.
Lord Slingsby-Craddock (*muttering protest*) Oh, I don't want to ...
Lady Slingsby-Craddock (*insistent*) Maple six-six-five-four-one- two-three.

Lord Slingsby-Craddock approaches the phone and lifts the receiver while Lady Slingsby-Craddock holds the base of the phone

Six-six-five-four-one-two-three.
Lady Slingsby-Craddock (*repeating the numbers as he dials*) Six-six-five-four-one-two-three.
Tweedy Lady And make it snappy.
Lord Slingsby-Craddock And make it snappy. Thank you. (*Muttering*) I don't know why the bally thing needs tuning. Bally thing's brand new.

Mint's phone rings

Scene C

Mint is still sitting reading the paper. The radio is playing. He answers the phone

Hallo. I want to speak to a piano tuner.

Mint cannot hear a word. He shakes his head

(*Shouting*) Piano tuner. If you'd stop playing that piano you'd hear me.

Mint indicates by gesture that he is to hold on a minute. Mint puts down the phone and goes to the radio

Bally chap's gone.

Mint switches off the radio. He returns to the phone. The kettle in the kitchen starts to whistle

I want to speak to a piano tuner.

Mint indicates for him to hold on

Tweedy Lady What's goin' on there?
Lord Slingsby-Craddock Bally fellow's playing a flute now.

Mint goes into the kitchen. He trips on the cat and brings a pile of saucepans down. He falls

Now he's playing the drums.

Mint manages to turn off the gas. He limps back to the phone, trying to coax the cat from under the chair with "Pussy" noises as he does so

(*Hearing these*) Eh?

Mint indicates he is now ready

(*Speaking rapidly*) Now listen here, my man, I want a piano tuner, and I want one in a hurry. Get out here as quick as you can. Craddock Grange—on the hill. Can't miss it. Have a look inside the thing. See what you can do. Make it snappy. Right? I'll pay you. Goodbye. (*He slams the phone down*)

Mint stands bemused. The Lights fade on him

That's settled his hash!

Lady Slingsby-Craddock Well done, Edward.

Lord Slingsby-Craddock (*pleased with himself*) Go for a stroll, eh?

Lady Slingsby-Craddock Oh yes. Let's go for a stroll.

Tweedy Lady Cracking idea.

Lord Slingsby-Craddock Just a short stroll. (*He whistles for his dog*) Panther—Panther, come here boy, come on boy. Come here, boy. Come on, Panther . . . Heel boy. Good dog.

An enormous dog approaches and all but flattens him

Lord and Lady Slingsby-Craddock and the Tweedy Lady go out

Scene D

Mint galvanizes into action, snatches up his bag, looks round the room, then goes out through the front door, slamming it behind him

He gets to his car, finds the starting handle and goes round to the front. He gives the engine a turn. Nothing happens. He runs back round to the driving seat. He adjusts the controls and runs back to crank. He gives the engine another turn. It fires and splutters but peters out before he can reach the controls

Mint, now getting desperate, dashes to and fro dementedly. Alternately cranking, running round and hurling himself into the driver's seat. But each time he is beaten. By the finish he is moving at tremendous speed and the whole sequence is speeded up. He gives up. He stands regarding his car. Silence

A Pedestrian enters on a bicycle. He dismounts. He is a weird-looking individual in a long raincoat, cloth cap and glasses. He is one of the helpful types. He stands beside Mint and surveys the situation

Mint indicates his problem. The Pedestrian takes the starting handle, steps forward and has a go. The Pedestrian suffers the same fate as Mint. Then a knowing look comes into his eyes. He produces a large spanner and disappears under the car. The klaxon horn sounds loudly on the car. The Pedestrian shoots out from under the car at incredible speed and stands upright, sucking his fingers

The Pedestrian indicates he is ready for another try. Mint climbs into the driving seat. He gives the Pedestrian the OK signal. The Pedestrian signals back. The Pedestrian cranks. The engine fires. As the engine revs up, the Pedestrian revolves on the end of the crank handle at great speed. It is some seconds before Mint sees him and comes to the rescue. He disengages the Pedestrian who continues to shake. They are both coughing with the smoke from the car

Mint runs back to the driving seat and climbs in. He waves and drives away

Scene E

Mint motors. He pulls on a pair of goggles and a hat and performs various hand signals. He narrowly misses someone or something and sounds his horn. He looks relieved. The Pedestrian overtakes him on the bicycle and waves

The Lights cross-fade to Cecil and Amanda. Cecil and Amanda walk in the grounds

Cecil I say, it's a jolly lovely day . . .
Amanda Yes, jolly lovely . . .
Cecil Yes . . .

They walk

(*Suddenly*) I say . . .
Amanda What?
Cecil Look!
Amanda What?
Cecil Ducks—ducks on a pond.
Amanda Yes . . .
Cecil Whole pond covered in ducks—all over it ducks . . .
Amanda Yes . . .
Cecil Whose are they?
Amanda Daddy's. They're Daddy's ducks.
Cecil I never knew he had ducks. I adore ducks, don't you?
Amanda Oh, yes.
Cecil Always had a soft spot for ducks for some reason. (*He hails them*) Hallo ducks!

Mint observes a pretty girl. He turns and wolf whistles. Mint wings something. He turns, raises his hat in apology, and continues

Cecil is crouching by the pond

Quack—quack—quack—I think they're hungry.
Amanda Oh, do come on, Cecil——
Cecil Hang on a tick, they're hungry. Quack—quack—don't have a slice of bread on you, do you?

Amanda No——
Cecil Quack—quack——
Amanda Oh, Cecil . . .
Cecil Quack!

Mint arrives in the grounds of Craddock Grange. The car bumps up and down a bit. The car stops suddenly with a jolt. Mint sits still for a moment gazing round, listening to the birds. Then he removes his goggles, stretches and inhales the air

Cecil and Amanda:

Cecil Ah—ha—there's some duckweed. Ducks simply adore duckweed. I heard that somewhere—hang on.
Amanda Oh Cecil——
Cecil Just . . . (*Straining*) Just—wait a tick while—I—get—it—and——

Splash. The ducks quack

Oh, I say—help!—I say . . .

Amanda goes unperturbed and unmoving. She looks away at the sky, she sighs deeply

Cut to Mint: He sighs deeply. He looks round for someone who will direct him. He appears to be alone. The sound of a motor mower attracts his attention. He walks to the source of the noise

An old rustic in a white straw hat and a long white coat is walking up and down the length of the stage, quite rapidly, behind a motor mower

The man passes Mint once or twice before Mint can catch his attention. When the Gardener does see Mint he nods cursorily but continues his task. Mint trots beside him explaining his mission. When the Gardener does reply his speech is a garbled rustic which is understood by neither Mint nor us

Gardener If it be the hall you be wanting, you best take the path straight up to the yew tree—turn left, then bear right at the summerhouse and then straight up past the marquee and the rose garden, till you get to the main drive and then straight on up and you can't miss it. And keep off the grass.

With a final glare the Gardener exits, leaving Mint alone

Scene F

Mint walks

Lord Slingsby-Craddock (*off*) Panther—put that man down—come back here!

Panther barks and growls somewhere in the distance

Cecil (*off*) Amanda! *Amanda*! I'm all soggy.
Lady Slingsby-Craddock (*off*) Whoo-hoo! Coming . . .
Tweedy Lady (*off*) This blasted rose is covered in greenfly—covered in . . .

Mint reaches the steps to the front door. He looks up at the enormous building, tidies himself and then pulls the front doorbell. He does a short little wander while he's waiting for the door to be opened. He goes to ring again, but as he does so, the door chimes deeply and distantly. He starts

Someone on the other side of the door spends a long time unfastening it. Finally, a Butler opens the door. He regards Mint. When he speaks, he has a plummy tenor voice

Butler Yes?

Mint indicates his intention. He mimes a piano being played furiously and opens his mouth to speak

(*Impassively*) Oh yes, Lord Craddock did mention . . . This way.

Mint steps inside. The Butler closes the door. The Butler begins to lead the way along a maze of passages which zig-zag across the stage. Each door they come to is mimed carefully. It creaks when opened and again when closed by Mint. Their footsteps echo on the floor. Thus the whole thing has a sort of rhythmic sequence which makes it both more comic and easier to achieve. Thus from the slam of the front door, things get underway. Say, six even footsteps, beat pause, door opens, beat pause, door closes, beat pause. Through the first door they go straight on, Mint following behind the Butler. At the second door they turn left. At the third door, as Mint turns to close it, he sees something, a picture on the wall. He stops

The Butler continues alone, to the fourth door, where he turns right and closes it behind him. On the fifth set the Butler continues alone, through another door, turning right again. Mint follows up the Butler, realizing he has been left behind, but turns left instead of right. The Butler continues, turns right again. Mint continues, turns left again. When they are through these doors without interrupting the rhythm, the Butler is aware that he has lost Mint. Mint has the feeling he has lost himself

The Butler goes along the passage to the seventh door, turns right again, in search of Mint. Mint goes along the passage to the door, and turns left. The Butler goes along the passage, retracing his steps now to find Mint. He turns left through the door. Mint goes along the passage, turns right through the door and heads in the direction of the front door

The Butler is now following Mint's earlier route. He turns left, through the door. Mint turns right. The Butler goes on and turns left again. Mint goes straight on to the front door. The Butler goes on and through the door, and he is back at the crossroads. Mint goes on to the front door. He blinks in the sunlight

A pause. The Butler stands bemused. Mint stands for a moment. Then shrugs and pulls at the doorbell. Pause. When it does ring it is very loud and the Butler starts. Mint stands. The Butler straightens himself, dismisses Mint from his mind and makes the three trips necessary to the front door. A little wearily. Straight on. Then right. Then straight on. He opens the front door. Mint and he regard each other for a minute. Mint apologetically raises his hat

The Butler seizes Mint and thrusts him inside. The Butler slams the front door, then pushing Mint in front of him he drives him at great speed towards the drawing-room; straight along one passage, through one door, straight along the next passage, turns left through the second door, along another passage, turns right through the third door and along a final passage. He opens the drawing-room door and closes it behind them. Mint stumbles into the room, finally released from the Butler's grip. The Butler stands with his back to the door, exhausted. A pause

Don't you dare ruddy well move from here.

He goes out

Scene G

Mint surveys his surroundings. He whistles silently, approvingly and fingers the upholstery of the armchairs. He shakes his head. He approaches the piano. He studies it and makes an approving face. He plays a single note. He winces and shakes his head. He plays three swift chords. More disapproval. He stands and regards his task for a moment

Amanda enters alone on the lawn carrying a deck chair which she sets up and sits down in. She has her sun hat, a sun top and glasses. She carries a cocktail which she is sipping through a straw. She lies back with her glass, eyes closed

Mint, as soon as she is established, decides to set to work. He removes his hat, wanders to the window and, in passing, sees Amanda but does not register. He moves back to the piano and begins to strike a note continuously, in the manner of piano tuners. Suddenly, Amanda's image registers on his brain. He plays a loud discord and runs back to the window. Mint waves and attempts to attract her attention, but although she is facing him, her eyes are closed and she does not notice him. Mint jumps up and down for a minute to no avail. He finally clambers on the piano stool and starts to climb on the piano. He treads on the keybord. A discord

This sound causes Amanda to look up. They stare at each other. Amanda looks startled. Mint, now shy, sits himself at the piano. He plays some sweeping chords and trills. Amanda sits back mildly amused. Mint smiles at her. His flashing chords culminate rather feebly in "Chopsticks" which makes her smile. He follows with snatches of increasingly passionate love songs. Amanda leans forward listening

Cecil enters with a box of chocolates which he presents to Amanda

She doesn't notice him. Cecil sees Mint through the french windows, scowls and thrusts the chocolates vigorously under Amanda's nose

Amanda (*returning her attention to Cecil*) Oh, wheee! Choccies!

Mint, seeing competition, glares at Cecil and thunders out the funeral march. Amanda smiles

Scene H

Lady Slingsby-Craddock and the Tweedy Lady stand in the doorway

Mint is suddenly aware of them. Mint's playing tails away to a few disconnected notes. Cecil enters the room by the french windows. Mint rises, stands by the piano and smiles at them, weakly. He indicates the piano. They stare at him stonily. Mint produces a tuning fork and twangs it loudly

Lady Slingsby-Craddock (*comprehending*) Ah, piano tuner chappie.
Tweedy Lady Piano tuner chappie.
Cecil (*with deep suspicion*) Piano tuner chappie—eh.

Mint suddenly finds them very amusing and has trouble containing his laughter. Cecil steps forward, angrily

Is it tuned?

Mint plays a note

Is that the best you can do? (*Cecil plays a note*) Excruciating!

Mint plays two notes simultaneously, twice. He is now annoyed. Cecil plays three notes, three times. Mint promptly tries to stop him with four from the bass end. They both move towards each other, Mint up the piano, Cecil down. They meet, almost nose to nose. They stop and regard each other, and look as though they might come to blows

Lady Slingsby-Craddock Steady on.
Tweedy Lady (*laughing*) Steady the buffs.

Mint steps aside. Cecil preens himself, glares at Mint and settles himself at the piano. Coughing from Lady Slingsby-Craddock and the Tweedy Lady. Cecil waits politely. Silence. He is about to start. Mint coughs. Cecil pauses pointedly. At last he starts to play "Für Elise" without much feeling or sensitivity and rather over-elaborately

Amanda (*from the garden*) Oh . . .

Mint moves in her direction

Cecil . . . how terrif!

Cecil smiles at her and closes his eyes. Mint eyes Cecil coldly. He looks put out. Mint looks round, the Tweedy Lady and Lady Slingsby-Craddock are both sitting, eyes closed with expressions of rapture

Mint sidles up to the bass end of the piano, unobserved. At a crucial point he adds a discordant note to Cecil's playing. Lady Slingsby-Craddock, the Tweedy Lady and Cecil all react, but Amanda doesn't appear to notice. Mint tries it again. This time Cecil's suspicions are aroused. He looks hard at Mint who puts on an innocent expression. The third time Cecil openly glares at Mint who shakes his head. Mint tries it again. Cecil is ready for him and slaps his hand, hard

Amanda rises and walks dreamily in from the garden. She pauses by the piano and stands close to Cecil and touches him. Mint leans over. She again ignores him. She goes and sits by Lady Slingsby-Craddock

Mint looks round furtively, then puts his hand inside the piano and starts tightening the strings. The music becomes shrill. All eyes on Cecil. He smiles apologetically but carries on playing. He looks carefully at the pedals, searching for the trouble, then glances inside the piano. Amanda draws his attention to Mint's hand. Cecil plays a heavy chord. Mint withdraws clutching his fingers

Lady Slingsby-Craddock Ssshhh!
Tweedy Lady Ssssshhh.
Amanda Oh, do shush.
Tweedy Lady Sit down, young man.
Lady Slingsby-Craddock Sit down.

They all close their eyes. Cecil strikes up the First Movement of "Moonlight Sonata". Mint looks around for a seat. There is none. He sits on the piano stool with his back to Cecil

Cecil (*craning his neck whilst still playing*) Do you mind?
Amanda (*opening her eyes*) Cecil.
Cecil Mmmm?
Amanda Mmm! Darling. (*She blows him a kiss. She closes her eyes*)

Mint bounces up and down on the stool in time to the music. Cecil pushes him off, with a backward shove. Cecil continues playing for a second. Mint suddenly swings him round on the revolving stool so that his back is to the keyboard. Mint plays a quick chorus of "Twelfth Street Rag"

Cecil swings back and pushes him away. He resumes "Moonlight Sonata". Mint jumps hard on his foot. Cecil hops away, agonized. Mint resumes "Twelfth Street Rag". Cecil recovering, infuriated, slams the lid down on Mint's fingers. Mint howls and leaps in the air. A silence, sudden and absolute. The ladies hold their breath. Cecil has grabbed Mint's shirt front and brought him to his feet. They stand nose to nose

Cecil Get out.
Tweedy Lady Hear hear.

Mint removes Cecil's hand from his shirt with considerable difficulty, quite slowly. He surveys the room with narrowed eyes. He walks slowly towards Amanda and looks her up and down. Amanda suppresses a scream. Then Mint walks backwards to the french windows, much in the manner of a cowboy. He picks up Cecil's large sunhat, holding it like a sombrero. All this silent and slowly

At the last moment, suddenly, unexpectedly and violently, Mint makes to rush at them, emits a terrible shriek and rushes off into the garden and exits

The remaining four react to this by leaping into a tight huddle where they remain for a second or two after his exit. Cecil at last steps forward

Amanda (*together*) Well done, Cecil.
Lady Slingsby-Craddock (*together*) Thank you, Cecil.
Tweedy Lady (*together*) Should have clouted him if you ask me.

Cecil (*wiping a hand across his brow*) I feel terrible.

He strides out

Amanda (*running after him*) Cecil, Cecil—don't go—wait for me—Cecil . . .

She goes

Tweedy Lady Shockin'
Lady Slingsby-Craddock Ghastly.
Tweedy Lady Poor show.
Lady Slingsby-Craddock Rum do.
Tweedy Lady No go.
Lady Slingsby-Craddock Shoddy business.
Tweedy Lady Awful.

Pause

Lady Slingsby-Craddock Do you play tennis?
Tweedy Lady Tennis?
Lady Slingsby-Craddock Yes.
Tweedy Lady Oh, *tennis*. Love to. Love to. Nothing like tennis, I always say, for clearing the air. Nothing like it. Good sport.
Lady Slingsby-Craddock Good.
Tweedy Lady Yes, jolly good sport.

She gives Lady Slingsby-Craddock a hearty slap

Lady Slingsby-Craddock reacts. They go out

Scene I

Lord Slingsby-Craddock enters alone. He is pottering in the garden. He whistles his dog

Lord Slingsby-Craddock Panther—Panther—come along boy. Heel . . . that's a good boy . . . good dog . . . (*He picks up a ball and shows it to the* *dog*) Here we are boy . . . fetch it boy . . . after it boy . . . (*He throws the ball with all his might*)

Sound of dog receding. Pause. There is a distant crash as the ball shatters a greenhouse

Lord Slingsby-Craddock shrugs and wanders off, resigned and not really perturbed

As he goes Mint enters

Neither see the other. Mint is evidently lost. He wears the large sun hat which he takes off, fans himself with and puts on again. He gazes in all directions in search of his car. He examines his feet. They are tired. He sits on a tree stump and removes a shoe. He whistles to himself

The large dog appears, Mint sees it and rises in alarm, abandoning his shoe. The dog seems unfriendly. Mint backs away, smiling fixedly and making doggy noises. The dog is evidently unimpressed. It approaches Mint's shoe. Mint tries to get his shoe back. First by coaxing the dog. This fails. He walks slowly over to it, looking unconcerned. He jumps back. He runs at the shoe. He runs back. Finally, he walks elaborately past it, as if going in a different direction. He then makes a sudden sideways grab. The dog catches hold of his trousers. Mint hops about

Lord Slingsby-Craddock enters

(*Seeing Mint*) Ah-ha.

Mint raises his hat with difficulty. Lord Slingsby-Craddock ambles across to Mint

Jolly nice to see you. Having a look at the grounds, are you? (*All this above the dog growling*) They're at their best at this time of year—(*very fiercely and loudly, suddenly to the dog*)—*Down boy* . . . So glad you could get down. Does my wife know you're here? (*To the dog*) *Heel boy*!

Mint reacts. The whole conversation is interspersed with these ferocious commands which always catch him unawares. The dog releases Mint and recedes

Have you met the other guests? *Panther*! I don't quite know where they'll all be. (*He takes Mint's arm*) I think they said something about tennis . . . *Panther, come back here!* Do you know the tennis courts? I'll show you. I'm going up that way . . . *Panther!* Come along, my boy. Hope you can swing a racket. *Panther!*

They go out

Scene J

Lady Slingsby-Craddock, the Tweedy Lady, Amanda and Cecil enter dressed for tennis. Merry chatter

Lady Slingsby-Craddock May be a bit rusty.
Tweedy Lady Same here. Same here. Need a bit of a limber.

Cecil cranks up the net while Amanda measures with her racket and his

Cecil Say when.
Amanda Up . . . up . . . whooaa!
Lady Slingsby-Craddock I don't know whether to wear my cardi or not.
Tweedy Lady Nonsense, Val. Gorgeous day.

Cecil and Amanda are holding hands and giggling together

Lady Slingsby-Craddock (*calling across to the court*) Cecil!
Cecil Hallo?
Lady Slingsby-Craddock I'll play with Amanda. You partner Mrs Grisley-Williams, will you dear?
Cecil Love to.
Tweedy Lady Burn the young blood at both ends, eh? (*She laughs*)

Nobody else does

Amanda (*with a squeal of alarm*) Oh but I can't play against Cecil. He's terribly, terribly good . . .
Lady Slingsby-Craddock Don't be silly darling.
Amanda Oh but I can't, Mummy, I can't.
Cecil I'm a bit off form this year anyway . . .
Amanda I can't, *can't*, CAN'T.
Cecil Shall we spin for service?
Lady Slingsby-Craddock Right-ho.
Cecil You call . . .
Amanda Smooth . . . no, rough . . . no, smooth.
Cecil I say, steady on. Rough. Rotten luck.
Lady Slingsby-Craddock We'll start this end.
Cecil Right.
Amanda I'll never be able to play. I'll never be able to . . .
Tweedy Lady Have a bit of a knock first, eh?
Lady Slingsby-Craddock Got the balls, Cecil?
Cecil Balls—yes. Coming over. Ready?

Cecil hits a ball over the net. Lady Slingsby-Craddock returns it to the Tweedy Lady. The Tweedy Lady hits the ball back with enormous force straight at Amanda. Amanda squeals and runs out of the way of it

Amanda Oh, Mrs Grisley, I say, steady on.
Lady Slingsby-Craddock Calm down, darling.
Cecil (*holding up another ball*) Ready?
Lady Slingsby-Craddock (*picking up a ball*) Right.

The knock-up starts in earnest. Lady Slingsby-Craddock and Cecil start it off by both hitting a ball over at once. The general impression of sight and sound co-ordination will be achieved if all the players play back and forth steadily and regularly. There are various cries of "sorry" "Oh dear", and squeals from Amanda

During the knock-up, Lord Slingsby-Craddock and Mint enter. They are deep in conversation and walk into the middle of the court, before they realize that they are under fire

Lord Slingsby-Craddock Who's winning?
Cecil Not playing yet. (*He stops*)
Tweedy Lady (*out of breath*) 'Bout time we did. No energy left soon.

The knock-up stops

Amanda (*flinging herself down on the ground and sprawling out*) I'm whacked.
Lord Slingsby-Craddock Have you met Mr—er ... Mr—er ... Mr ...

Mint waves and pulls his hat further down over his eyes

Lady Slingsby-Craddock Hallo ... excuse us. We'll try and give you a knock later on.
Amanda (*rising*) Who's serving?
Cecil (*bouncing a ball*) We are. Ready?
Amanda (*in alarm*) Oh, you're not serving to me?
Cecil Looks like it. Ready?
Amanda Oh, Cecil ...

Cecil prepares to serve. He is a stylish player

Oh, oh ... (*She jumps about in anticipation*)

Cecil serves. The ball zips past Amanda

Oh!
Cecil (*pleased*) Bad luck.
Lord Slingsby-Craddock (*who has assumed the mantle of umpire, but who is, incidentally, looking elsewhere*) Fault.
Cecil (*aghast*) Fault?
Lord Slingsby-Craddock (*firmly*) Fault.

Mint nods confirmation. Cecil glowers. He serves again, slower

Amanda (*returning the ball*) Wheeee!

She has lobbed the ball straight to the Tweedy Lady who shapes herself for a smash

Tweedy Lady (*loudly*) Mine!
Lady Slingsby-Craddock (*anticipating the smash; to Amanda*) Stay there. (*She runs for the base line*)

The Tweedy Lady smashes with customary vigour. The ball hits Lady Slingsby-Craddock in the small of her back

AAaaaahh!
Tweedy Lady Sorry!
Cecil I say ...
Amanda Mummy!

Lady Slingsby-Craddock, clutching her back, reels in a small circle. Amanda runs to her

Lord Slingsby-Craddock Sliced. Sliced the smash. (*He shakes his head*)

Cecil, recovering himself, bounds over the net and helps Amanda with Lady Slingsby-Craddock

Lady Slingsby-Craddock All right. I'll be all right.
Tweedy Lady (*from the other side of the net, breezily*) Sorry, Val. Luck of the game and all that.
Lady Slingsby-Craddock (*with a watery smile*) Yes.
Cecil Have a sit down.
Amanda Have a lie down.
Tweedy Lady What about the game?
Amanda Oh dear. Daddy will you play?
Lord Slingsby-Craddock Not bally likely. Not insured like your mother.
Tweedy Lady What about you, Mr Whatsit? Make up a four, eh?

Mint looks doubtful

Amanda Oh go on Mr Whatnot. Be a sport, Mr Whatnot. Please Mr Whatnot—just to please me——

Mint gives her a leer

Oh.

Mint picks up a racket

Tweedy Lady Bravo!
Lady Slingsby-Craddock (*going off*) I'll see about tea.

Lady Slingsby-Craddock goes

Amanda	(*together*)	Bye, Mummy.
Tweedy Lady		See you, Val.
Cecil		So long.

Tweedy Lady Start again.
Cecil (*who is staring suspiciously at Mint*) Haven't we met before?

Mint pulls his hat down

No I thought not.

They take up their positions

Amanda 'Fraid I'm not awfully good, Mr Whatnot.

Mint continues to fix her with his smile. Amanda looks disconcerted

Cecil Ready, Mr—er?

Mint wrenches his attention away from Amanda

Cecil serves to Amanda. Amanda returns to Cecil. Cecil returns to Mint who misses, clumsily

Oh bad luck. (*He smiles at Mint*)

Amanda giggles. Mint looks annoyed. He braces himself

Lord Slingsby-Craddock Fifteen-love.

Cecil changes courts

Cecil Ready Mr—er . . . ?

Mint crouches in a cricket stance

Cecil goes to serve to Mint. Disconcerted by his attitude, he checks himself. Repeat business

Are you quite sure you're ready?

Mint nods

Oh!

Mint springs to meet it, holding his racket two-handed like a cricket bat. He hits the ball like a bullet, straight back at Cecil. Cecil ducks just in time. The ball hits the wire with a loud clang

Tweedy Lady Keep it in the parish.
Amanda Well hit, Mr Whatnot.

Cecil still can't get over the force with which the ball came back. Mint looks pleased with himself

Lord Slingsby-Craddock Thirty-love.

Mint is deflated

Amanda We're losing, Mr Whatnot. Better pull our socks up.

Mint gives her a confident smile and spits on his hands

Cecil serves to Amanda. Amanda returns to the Tweedy Lady. The Tweedy Lady hammers at Mint. Mint manages a return to Cecil. Cecil back to Amanda. Amanda back to the Tweedy Lady who is beaten

Tweedy Lady Ah, too old for that one. Good shot.
Lord Slingsby-Craddock Thirty-fifteen.

Cecil serves to Mint who waves both his arms violently as Cecil is up on his toes. Cecil mis-hits. The ball knocks off Lord Slingsby-Craddock's hat. He protests vigorously. Cecil apologizes

Second service.
Cecil (*looking pointedly at Mint*) Are you ready now, Mr—er . . . ?

Cecil serves again to Mint. Mint runs forward. Cecil and the Tweedy Lady retreat and disappear from view. Mint deliberately and gently taps the ball over the net

Tweedy Lady Shot.
Amanda Oh, well done, Mr Whatnot.

Lord Slingsby-Craddock Thirty-all.

Cecil serves to Amanda. Amanda returns and beats him

Amanda Oh, wheeee! We're winning.
Lord Slingsby-Craddock Thirty-forty.
Tweedy Lady (*thumping Cecil*) Brace up partner.

Cecil looks annoyed

Cecil serves a scorcher to Mint. Mint gets nowhere near it

Cecil (*without a trace of sympathy*) Bad luck.
Lord Slingsby-Craddock Deuce.
Tweedy Lady Well served.

Cecil serves to Amanda. Mint, anxious to make amends, intercepts the ball before it reaches her and returns with a high lob

Amanda Hey!
Tweedy Lady *Mine*!

She runs to intercept the lob which is clearly Cecil's. She knocks him sideways in her onrush. This impedes her and she fails to reach it

Oh. Must look out of the way, man.
Cecil (*lamely*) Sorry.
Lord Slingsby-Craddock 'Vantage—Mr Whatsisname.
Tweedy Lady Shouldn't have missed that.

Cecil serves to Mint. Mint returns to the Tweedy Lady. The Tweedy Lady to Amanda. Amanda returns to Cecil. Cecil to Mint. Mint hits the ball high in the air above Cecil and the Tweedy Lady

Mine . . .
Cecil Mine . . .

While the ball is in the air Mint runs round the net and behind Cecil and the Tweedy Lady. As the ball falls between them he jumps and returns it

Lord Slingsby-Craddock Out! Game Mr Whatsisname.

Mint runs to the net and puts his arms in the air, smiling. A stony silence. The others look coldly at him. Mint's smile fades

Tweedy Lady Poor show.
Cecil Poor show indeed. About it for today.
Amanda Call it a day. Yes.
Tweedy Lady Up for tea.
Cecil Good idea.
Amanda Tea, yes.

The three go out

Mint is left standing crestfallen. Lord Slingsby-Craddock sits ruminatively on his shooting stick and surveys the court. A pause

Lord Slingsby-Craddock You finished playing?

Mint nods

Oh well. Go and have some tea, then. Eh?

Scene K

Lady Slingsby-Craddock enters with a small table

Lady Slingsby-Craddock (*calling brightly*) Tea everybody!

The others enter. Cecil carries a chair and a cakestand. Amanda carries two chairs. Both come from the opposite direction. The Tweedy Lady enters behind Lady Slingsby-Craddock carrying two chairs

The next few minutes is taken up with furious activity. The following is intended merely as covering dialogue

I thought we'd have it out of doors. Sandwiches always taste nicer in the open. Will you all get yourself a chair and sit where you like. I'm going to ask you all to help yourselves if you don't mind. I've had labels put on the sandwiches so you can't mistake them. I hope you all take tea. If not there's orange squash for those who want it.

Cecil . . . No, I was coming out of this concealed turning straight on to the A-seventeen and this maniac comes whipping round, absolutely flat out. I ran clean on to the grass verge and missed him by inches. Took the paint off one wing. I was absolutely seething, I can tell you. Just had the bodywork re-done. Cost me the best part of twenty quid. "Look here", I said, "who the devil do you think you are? Don't you bother to read signposts. They're not put there just for fun you know." Well, this chap was as rude as blazes . . .

Amanda I shall be awfully ill having tea on top of tennis and I do hate it in the open air anyway. We ought to do what Jennifer Sidebotham's parents do, Mummy. They have a marquee. Then the wind doesn't blow the napkins all over the garden. I mean I think sitting out here in a howling gale sipping tea is absolutely insane. I mean, nobody really enjoys it. It's just convention. I think we should all be outrageous and have tea indoors, just for once . . .

Tweedy Lady Thundering good game polo. My late husband and I used to play together. Ever played polo, Val? Ought to get Edward on to a pony. Do him good. Always loafin' around the garden. Kill him off quicker than anything. I'd play only I'm too heavy for it. Ruddy pony'd collapse, more's the pity. Nothing like gallopin' round a field swingin' at a ball. Much healthier than huntin'. Spend too much time pickin' yourself out of insanitary ditches for my likin'. Damn foxes. No consideration . . .

Lord Slingsby-Craddock If I were you, I'd grab a chair, sit down and eat. And keep as far away as you can from that Mrs Grisley-Williams. She's got an appetite like a bally rhinoceros . . .

During this: Mint goes to help Lady Slingsby-Craddock with the table, staying with it up by the entrance, till she indicates for him to put it down. Lady Slingsby-Craddock goes C *and takes a chair from Amanda who crosses up. Cecil follows her and deposits the cakestand. Lord Slingsby-Craddock follows Mint for part of his journey, meets the Tweedy Lady and takes a chair from her. Lady Slingsby-Craddock distributes side plates to all but Mint. The company, with the exception of Mint, who has no chair anyway, range themselves in a line across the stage facing the table with Mint behind it. The conversation keeps up*

Tweedy Lady Bit of a hurricane blowing here. (*She is shouting above the babble*)

Amanda (*also shouting*) It's terribly draughty, Mummy.

They are all holding on to their hats and giving the impression of a fairly high wind

Lady Slingsby-Craddock It's only the sun gone in.

Lord Slingsby-Craddock (*testily*) I wish you'd use your bally nouse, Val. We're all catching pneumonia out here.

Lady Slingsby-Craddock Well let's all move round then. (*To Mint*) Would you mind, Mr—er . . . ? (*She indicates the table*)

The party move their chairs to face the other way, in a body. Mint obligingly carries the table round them, since there is no space between them. He sets it down

Amanda It's worse here.

Tweedy Lady It's coming from the sou' sou' west, Val. Get the whole blast of the beastly thing if you face west.

Lord Slingsby-Craddock Blow your sandwiches down your bally throat.

Cecil I say . . .

Tweedy Lady Want to face east. East that way.

Lady Slingsby-Craddock Oh, very well. Would you mind, Mr—er . . . ? (*She indicates the table*)

The party swing their chairs through ninety degrees. Mint staggers round the table

Lord Slingsby-Craddock Don't want to worry you but now we are facing west.

Tweedy Lady This is east.

Lord Slingsby-Craddock If this is east my ancestors are up the bally creek. That's the west wing, woman.

Amanda (*wearily*) Move round.

They move round. Mint reels round them with the table and sets it down. He glares

Lady Slingsby-Craddock Thank you so much, Mr—er . . . ? Poor man, he must be exhausted carrying that table round and round . . . Now, is everybody quite happy?

Chorus of assent

The order of seating at this moment should be: Amanda, Cecil, Lady Slingsby-Craddock, Tweedy Lady, Lord Slingsby-Craddock. All in a straight line. Mint stands alone by the table. General covering conversation breaks out afresh

Lady Slingsby-Craddock Do sit down, Mr—er ... ? You look quite lost standing there.

Mint looks round vainly

Have you been in the rose garden, Emily?

Tweedy Lady Rather. Stood there sniffing my lungs out. Gorgeous, Val, simply gorgeous. Wish I could grow 'em like that. All mine are such stunted little things. I said to Harold, you know, my man, I said prune 'em man, for heaven's sake prune 'em. Snipping away like some ladies' hairdresser. Roses got no respect for pansies.

Lady Slingsby-Craddock I don't think it's all pruning ...

Tweedy Lady Ninety per cent, surely. Ninety per cent.

Lady Slingsby-Craddock We're very lucky with our soil, I'm told. Something to do with the clay ...

Tweedy Lady Oh, Lord's sake, Val. Soil's soil. Makes no difference. All this scientific eyewash about sandstone belts. Just a cover up for damned incompetent gardening, that's all. My husband used to say—earth is what you make it ...

Lady Slingsby-Craddock Yes, I suppose you're right. I must say though we're very lucky ...

Amanda (*simultaneously*) Do you know who I saw on Thursday?

Cecil No? Go on?

Amanda Janet thingummybob... from the Gables ...

Cecil Good heavens! I thought she'd gone to Tanganyika with her brother.

Amanda Janet thingummybob?

Cecil Yes, gone to Africa I thought.

Amanda What brother?

Cecil Whose?

Amanda Janet thingummybob's?

Cecil Has she got a brother? Good Lord, I never knew. After all these years ...

Amanda No, she hasn't.

Cecil Hasn't?

Amanda No.

Cecil Then who are we talking about?

Amanda Janet thingummybob.

Cecil Janet thingummybob ... just a second ... hang on a minute ... no ... I don't think I know her. I was thinking of that Doris girl. The one whose brother got malaria and had fits over tea ... sure you don't mean her. She had a brother ...

Amanda I know, silly, I was nearly engaged to him.

Cecil Really? To that chap. Fits and all. Pretty bad social stigma, bit off ...

Amanda They weren't fits. They were seizures. Poor chap ...

During this, things are happening. The conversation, though, continues smoothly through it. Mint, instructed by Lady Slingsby-Craddock to sit down, wanders behind the chairs, searching for a seat. Lord Slingsby-Craddock, who takes no part in the conversation but sits moodily munching, rises suddenly and crosses to the table to help himself. Mint seeing his vacant chair sits on it. Just before Lord Slingsby-Craddock turns back from the table Cecil rises and comes to the table. Lord Slingsby-Craddock glances round absently, sees Cecil's as the only empty chair, crosses and sits down. Cecil returns to the chairs with a plate of sandwiches, ignores Mint and offers one to the Tweedy Lady who declines and rises to help herself. Cecil offers a sandwich to Lady Slingsby-Craddock, who accepts, Lord Slingsby-Craddock and Amanda briefly, who decline. Cecil sits in the Tweedy Lady's chair. Amanda rises to the table. The Tweedy Lady still deep in conversation with Lady Slingsby-Craddock sits on Amanda's chair

Where are the salmon ones, Mummy?

Lady Slingsby-Craddock (*interrupted*) There dear. (*She rises, still talking to the Tweedy Lady*)

Lady Slingsby-Craddock finds the sandwiches for Amanda, lingers, to tidy up the plates. Amanda, unthinkingly, sits on Lady Slingsby-Craddock's chair. Lady Slingsby-Craddock glances round for a seat. Mint chooses that precise moment to rise and pick up a sandwich he has dropped. Lady Slingsby-Craddock spots his empty chair and sits on it. Mint stands. The conversation continues

(*To Lord Slingsby-Craddock*) Are you all right, darling?

Lord Slingsby-Craddock Haven't had such an uncomfortable meal since I was in the army.

Lady Slingsby-Craddock Oh don't be such an old stick-in-the-mud.

Cecil Bit like living under canvas, eh, sir?

Lord Slingsby-Craddock Without the canvas.

Cecil Reminds me of manœuvres we had during our basic down on Salisbury Plain. Pretty draughty spot . . .

Lord Slingsby-Craddock Worst meal I ever had was in September, nineteen fifteen. Lousy food, appalling conditions . . .

Lady Slingsby-Craddock Edward . . .

Cecil We were keeping out of the wind behind the farmhouse, I deployed my chaps all over the place . . .

Lord Slingsby-Craddock I was having a word with my sergeant. Look here, sergeant, I said, can't you do something about the quality of these beans? Suddenly bang . . . (*He makes an expansive gesture*)

Cecil The idiot commanding the enemy suddenly decided to attack . . . rat-tat-tat-tat . . .

Lord Slingsby-Craddock Beans all over the shop. Heavy guns. The Hun sneaked them up . . .

Mint is becoming enthralled. The ladies resigned, listen politely. Each man begins to compete with the other in graphic description

Cecil Thunderflash, bang right by us. Blanks going off left right and centre . . . bang, bang, bang.
Lord Slingsby-Craddock Grenades, boom . . . mortar shells, big fellows . . . crrrummphhh!
Cecil We spread out . . . rat-tat-tat-tat . . . bang . . .
Lord Slingsby-Craddock Woof . . . woof . . . whole place was a living hell . . . boom . . . boom . . .
Cecil Splat . . . splat . . .
Lord Slingsby-Craddock Cruummph . . .
Cecil Bang . . .
Lord Slingsby-Craddock Digger . . . digger . . . digger . . .
Cecil Rat-tat-tat-tat . . .
Lord Slingsby-Craddock (*whistling*) Bang . . .
Mint (*joining in with enthusiasm*) Fizz . . . fizzz . . . fizzz . . .
Cecil Neeeeooowww!
Lord Slingsby-Craddock Sppp luunnk!
Mint Ber-doing, ber-doing, ber-doing . . .

Real war noises creep in under this

Cecil **Lord Slingsby-Craddock** **Mint**	(*together*)	Ow-ow-ow-ow-ow-ow-ow-ow . . . Woof . . . woof . . . woof . . . woof . . . Neee-takertaker . . . neeetaker taker . . .
Cecil **Lord Slingsby-Craddock** **Mint**	(*together*)	Gerdong, gerdong, gerdong . . . BOOM—brummph, BOOM—brumph . . . Bur-bur-bur-bur-bur-bur-bur-bur . . .
Cecil **Lord Slingsby-Craddock** **Mint**	(*together*)	Ack-ack-ack-ack-ack-ack-ack . . . Zeeow, zeeow, zeeeow . . . Bam-bam, bam-bam, bam-bam . . .

The Lights have changed to a dream-like colour. Everyone has risen. The men to make their stories more graphic, the women because the whole thing is getting a bit out of hand. Suddenly there comes the sound of an enormous shell, whistling as it descends

Tweedy Lady (*above the din, in alarm*) I say—look out everybody!
Lord Slingsby-Craddock Take cover!

The whole party, with cries of panic, flee up one end of the stage. Each takes a chair and Mint takes the table. They build a rough barricade. Lady Slingsby-Craddock however panics and runs round with her chair distant from the others

Lady Slingsby-Craddock Help! Help!
Tweedy Lady Val, for heaven's sake . . .
Lord Slingsby-Craddock Get down, woman. Get down . . .

Lady Slingsby-Craddock flings herself flat. So do the others. Just in time. An enormous explosion. Silence

Tweedy Lady Near thing, that . . .

Cecil All clear now I suppose . . .

He rises. A burst of machine-gun fire

Lord Slingsby-Craddock Get your head down, man!

Cecil throws himself flat

Lady Slingsby-Craddock Help!
Amanda Mummy!
Tweedy Lady Keep down.
Lord Slingsby-Craddock Valerie!
Lady Slingsby-Craddock (*calling*) Yes.
Lord Slingsby-Craddock Don't move from there!
Amanda We can't leave Mummy.
Lord Slingsby-Craddock Quiet a minute!
Amanda But, Daddy——
Lord Slingsby-Craddock Quiet in the ranks there. (*A ferocious command*) Going to take a recce. (*He sticks his head over the top cautiously*)

Machine-gun fire. He ducks down smartly

Hand me a bun.

The Tweedy Lady does so. Lord Slingsby-Craddock pulls the pin out of it with his teeth like a grenade and tosses it in the direction of the enemy. An explosion

That'll keep 'em quiet for a bit.
Lady Slingsby-Craddock Help!
Cecil All right, we're coming.
Tweedy Lady Who is?
Cecil Sir! I volunteer . . .
Amanda Oh, Cecil . . .
Lord Slingsby-Craddock Good chap. We'll give you covering fire. Pass the cress rolls.
Tweedy Lady Very stout gesture, young man. Good luck.

Romantic 1940s music: solo spot

Cecil If I don't come back, Amanda, spare a thought for me, now and then . . .
Amanda You'll be back darling. I know you will . . .
Cecil Amanda!

They embrace. The music fades

Lord Slingsby-Craddock Seems fairly clear now. When you're ready.
Cecil Right.
Lord Slingsby-Craddock Best of luck, old chap.
Tweedy Lady Pecker up.
Amanda I'm waiting, darling.
Cecil So long.
Lord Slingsby-Craddock Ready, Valerie?
Lady Slingsby-Craddock (*weakly*) Yes.

Lord Slingsby-Craddock Ready—fire!

They all hurl cress rolls. A series of explosions

(*During this*) Off you go, Chappie.

Cecil leaps over the top. Machine-gun bullets fly. Cecil leaps back again

Cecil Bit dangerous. Think I'll hang on a bit.
Amanda (*disappointed*) Oh, Cecil.
Cecil Said I'd be back.
Lord Slingsby-Craddock You won't get the bally VC for that.
Tweedy Lady Bit of a feeble gesture, what?

Mint has produced a white pocket handkerchief. He silences them with his hand. He stands up and waves the handkerchief

Lord Slingsby-Craddock What the devil are you doing man?
Tweedy Lady The fellow's surrendering . . .
Amanda I say, a coward . . .

Mint steps over the barricade. He smiles in the direction of the enemy, still holding the white flag in one hand, the other hand behind his back. Drumming

Lord Slingsby-Craddock Come back here.
Tweedy Lady Call yourself an Englishman.
Cecil Coward!
Amanda Coward!

They all "Ssss!" him. Mint, unperturbed, walks to the middle of the battlefield. He smiles at the enemy. He holds out his other hand with something in it, takes a bite out of it, inviting them to catch it. Then he tosses it gently to them and throws himself flat. An explosion

Mint runs to Lady Slingsby-Craddock and picks her up and carries her slowly across the stage. The sounds of a vast crowd cheering dementedly. "Land of Hope and Glory" is played. Lord Slingsby-Craddock steps forward to meet Mint, Amanda behind him. The Tweedy Lady and Cecil cheer from a distance. Mint presents Lord Slingsby-Craddock with Lady Slingsby-Craddock, takes one pace back and salutes. Lord Slingsby-Craddock embraces Lady Slingsby-Craddock who then retires with Cecil and the Tweedy Lady and takes up the cheering

Lord Slingsby-Craddock steps forward and there is a short ceremony of hand-shaking and saluting. Lord Slingsby-Craddock steps back. Amanda dashes forward and embraces Mint. He takes her hand and they step out on to a sort of balcony, isolated from the others. Mint and Amanda acknowledge the cheers alone. Suddenly Mint turns to her. They gaze into each other's eyes. Then they kiss. A long kiss

Suddenly the Lights fade on them, the cheering stops abruptly. The garden lighting returns, revealing the others seated as before. Amanda is now holding a plate of sandwiches which she is offering to Mint. The others are talking

Amanda I said would you like another anchovy sandwich, Mr—er . . . ?

Mint regards her for an instant

Lord Slingsby-Craddock And so we never got the meal. Had to eat chocolate in a pot-hole till someone dug us out, only consolation was that the Hun didn't get a meal either . . . (*He fades away*)

Mint is still in his dream. He seizes Amanda, draws her to him, plate and all and kisses her with nearly as much ardour as before. After an initial squeak, she yields. The others look on in amazement. Cecil rises. Stupefied. They part and look at each other

Lord Slingsby-Craddock (*breaking the spell*) Would you care for some more tea, Mr—er . . . ?

Mint shakes his head. Suddenly embarrassed, Amanda avoids all eyes. She hurries to the exit

Amanda Excuse me. (*Her voice is unsteady*) Getting a bit chilly.

She smiles nervously at the assembly, shoots a sidelong glance at Mint and exits

Pause

Lord Slingsby-Craddock Yes, it is a bit nippy. Shall we move inside?
Tweedy Lady (*staring at Mint*) Good idea.

Lord Slingsby-Craddock prepares to take the table off. Lady Slingsby-Craddock picks up two chairs, so does the Tweedy Lady

Cecil (*to Lord Slingsby-Craddock*) Can I help . . .
Lord Slingsby-Craddock (*pointedly*) No, no, no . . .

He goes off with the table

Lady Slingsby-Craddock (*following him; conversationally*) Yes, we've had the best of the day, I think.
Tweedy Lady Yes, the best bit's gone . . . (*Aside to Cecil loudly*) Do your stuff.

They exit

Mint and Cecil are left

Scene L

Balletic sequence. Cecil looks at Mint for a moment. He moves towards him as if to speak, then picks up a chair. He stands holding it. Mint walks slowly over towards him and picks up the cakestand. They stand there like two aggressors. Mint makes a sudden move

Cecil turns and runs. A crash

Mint stands for a moment. Waltz music. Mint dances with the cakestand

Lord Slingsby-Craddock enters and regards him

Mint, with his eyes still closed, stops deep in meditation. Lord Slingsby-Craddock takes hold of the cakestand. They waltz together. They stop, they laugh

Lord Slingsby-Craddock Has anyone showed you your room?

Mint shakes his head

Follow me.

They are in the room in an instant. It is set in one corner of the stage

This is it. Faces east. Gets the sun in the morning if you're up in time. Otherwise you've had it. Dinner at eight.

Lord Slingsby-Craddock goes out

Mint explores his room. Bounces on the bed. Looks at his watch. Mint then lies on the bed, turns off the light and goes to sleep

ACT II

Scene M

Music

Mint opens the closet door. A bundle drops in on him. It contains a dinner jacket and tie. He examines it for a second. He produces a shoe brush from his inner pocket and starts to polish his shoes rhythmically

The Lights come up in the room next to his in the other corner of the stage. Cecil is dressing for dinner in dinner jacket etc. He starts to hum the rhythm of Mint's shoe brushing. Some tune that can easily be sung as a round, say, "Frère Jacques"

As soon as Cecil has completed his chorus, the Lights come up in the far corner on Lady Slingsby-Craddock sitting at the dressing-table in her room bejewelling herself. She is humming "Frère Jacques"

Finally the Lights come up on Amanda who is changing in her room. She joins in the humming. Each, though, is unconscious of the other

Mint sees Amanda who is struggling with the zip of her dress. Amanda sees Mint. Their eyes meet. He reaches out a hand as if to help with the zip. She moves away. He does likewise. They come together again at their respective windows. He smiles. She smiles. He waves. She waves. He blows her a kiss. She blows him a kiss

Cecil has at this point been looking out of the window. He sees Amanda blowing a kiss, but does not see Mint who is out of his line of vision. Amanda sees Cecil. Cecil blows Amanda a kiss. Amanda covering up her previous action, blows Cecil a kiss. Mint blows a kiss back to Amanda

Lady Slingsby-Craddock, who at this point has moved to the window, sees Mint's kiss but is unable to see Amanda. Lady Slingsby-Craddock coyly blows a kiss to Mint. Cecil blows a kiss to Lady Slingsby-Craddock. An orgy of kiss blowing breaks out. It stops suddenly as each party realizes they are not alone. Amanda and Lady Slingsby-Craddock simultaneously look out of their windows, leaning out, and see each other. They regard each other, then the two men. They withdraw. Then both somewhat huffily draw their curtains. Both rooms Black-out

Cecil and Mint lean out of their respective windows and look at each other. A long pause. Mint blows Cecil a kiss. Cecil withdraws angrily, draws his curtains. His room fades out

Mint withdraws, holds up the dinner jacket, regards it, shrugs. Mint puts on the dinner jacket over his clothes. It is made for a different shaped man so it fits easily. He studies himself in the mirror, nods with satisfaction and vacates his room.

Mint exits

SCENE N

Meanwhile the Butler and a Maid enter carrying an oblong table of some length

They set it down centre stage. It is covered with an immense white tablecloth which reaches within a few inches of the floor on all sides. It is set with an enormous number of knives, forks and spoons of varying shapes and sizes. Also five wine glasses and perhaps two candelabra of similar dressing to indicate an opulent table

As they are doing this, Amanda enters and watches them with disinterest

The Butler and Maid exit

Amanda crosses to the table and absently straightens some knives and forks

Mint enters and stops dead as he sees her

She turns. A romantic look. Mint moves to Amanda, slowly. Their eyes never leave each other

The Butler enters with a chair

Mint shoots away from Amanda back to the other side of the room and looks away. So does she

The Butler places the chair at one end of the table, then exits

Mint and Amanda look at each other again. They move together as before

The Maid enters with another chair

Mint moves away, as before

The Maid sets the chair at the other end of the table, then exits

Mint moves to Amanda with a good deal more speed than before. Before they can touch . . .

The Butler is back with a bench which he sets to one side of the table. He exits

Mint at the other end of the room again takes a running jump at Amanda

The Maid enters with a bench. She sets it on the other side of the table

Mint walks over to the table. He stares at it, sees all the seating is in place. He and Amanda walk round the table from different sides, towards each other. Incredulous, their hands go out to each other and meet. Mint draws her to him, takes a quick look at all the doors. They go slowly into a kiss. The Lights change. Soft music. They waltz

The Butler enters with a menu. He is now a head waiter. He approaches Mint deferentially

He leads them to a corner of the table. He presents Mint with the menu. It is enormous. Mint makes a show of ordering

The Waiter withdraws

Amanda looks adoringly at Mint

The Butler enters with a very large bottle

The Butler pours a little wine into Mint's glass. He savours it, tosses the rest over his shoulder and nods. The Butler pours two glasses

The Butler withdraws

They toast each other

The Maid enters and dances a furious Spanish dance. She tosses Mint a rose

Mint and Amanda join in

The Maid withdraws

Mint takes Amanda by the hand. They rise and walk away from the table and sit in a corner. They are at the Opera

A spot comes up on the Maid singing the final bars of a Wagnerian duet. She is joined by the Butler who has the tenor role

Mint and Amanda fan themselves with programmes. Affectionate looks pass between them. The opera concludes. They applaud mildly

The Maid and Butler withdraw

Mint and Amanda rise. They are on the beach. There are seagulls and sea noises. They trip gaily down the beach with the sea breezes in their hair, like an advert for something or other, pause together, gaze into each other's eyes and embrace. They are now in the same position as when they started to dream. The whole business reaches a glorious Hollywood climax

It is shattered by a deafening gong sounded by the Butler, announcing dinner. The Maid holds the gong with difficulty

Mint and Amanda separate

Lady Slingsby-Craddock enters with Cecil. Lord Slingsby-Craddock follows

Lady Slingsby-Craddock Ah you're here. (*She sweeps over to Mint and takes his hand*) We thought for a dreadful moment we'd lost you, Mr—er . . . ?

Cecil has moved to Amanda

Do sit down everybody.

Lord Slingsby-Craddock has already done so. Mint heads for the seat next to Amanda. Cecil is already there. Mint sits on the other side of her. The three of them are thus squashed uncomfortably on one side of the table

Oh—er . . . Mr—er . . . ? Would you mind sitting over here? Think it'd be a bit less of a squash. I want you to sit next to me because I'm dying to have a chat with you.

Mint rises and reluctantly goes to the other side of the table. He glares at Cecil who smiles

That's better.

Mint sits opposite Amanda, leans over and stares at her. Cecil quietly moves the candelabra between them

Cecil You're looking jolly lovely this evening Amanda, if you don't mind me saying so.
Amanda Thank you, Cecil.
Cecil Jolly lovely.
Lord Slingsby-Craddock (*belching quietly to himself*) Bally cucumber sandwiches.

The Butler enters followed by the Maid who pushes a trolley with soup on it

Lady Slingsby-Craddock Ah, Herbert. Good-evening.
Butler Evening, milady.

He begins to serve the soup, starting with Lady Slingsby-Craddock then Amanda and round, Mint being served last

Lord Slingsby-Craddock Why the devil did we have cucumber sandwiches at teatime? Completely finished me . . .
Lady Slingsby-Craddock It's your own fault . . .
Lord Slingsby-Craddock Rubbish.

A silence falls as they all bury themselves in their soup. Mint has difficulty in finding the right implement. He checks with the others and finally gets hold of the soup spoon. He puts his rejects in his pocket. He is about to drink when he sees Lady Slingsby-Craddock looking at him. She blows him a coy kiss and nods. Mint smiles awkwardly and nods back. Lady Slingsby-Craddock smiles adoringly at him and blows another kiss. Mint transfers his spoon and is in the process of blowing one back when he finds the others are looking at him. He turns the gesture into a wave in the Butler's direction

The Butler nods and moves in. Mint smiles at Lord Slingsby-Craddock. The Butler removes Mint's plate leaving him with the spoon. Mint takes in the empty space and waves his soup spoon vaguely in the air wondering where to put it. Finally he slips it inside his jacket

The Maid deposits another plate in front of Mint. The fish course. The Maid exits with the trolley

Mint studies it. He selects a knife and fork, rejects them as unsuitable and puts them in his pocket. He selects two others and does the same with them. He finally finds a suitable pair. The others finish their soup. The Butler moves in to clear the plates, which he does rapidly. This includes Mint's uneaten fish

The Maid enters with the trolley now laden with four fish and one steak for Mint

Cecil (*as he finishes his soup*) That was jolly nice soup . . .
Lady Slingsby-Craddock Did you like it?
Cecil Never tasted anything like it before. What do you call it?
Lady Slingsby-Craddock Ah well, it's something rather special. It hasn't really got a name. Edward calls it Cook's Concoction . . .

Lord Slingsby-Craddock hiccups. The Maid is serving fish

Thank you, Agnes. I hope you all like Dover Sole. I'm afraid it's very selfish of me, but I adore it. Of course, it doesn't agree with Edward at all . . .

Lord Slingsby-Craddock glares. The Butler serves the wine

(*As he does so*) Thank you, Herbert.

The Butler has now reached Mint and starts to pour the wine. He pauses as Lady Slingsby-Craddock speaks to him

Herbert, I think we'll have coffee in the blue drawing-room this evening.
Butler Yes, milady.

Mint, during this, has drained his glass. The Butler begins to fill his glass again

Lord Slingsby-Craddock And Herbert . . .
Butler Yes, milord?
Lord Slingsby-Craddock Make sure all the doors are locked tonight. I found one in the east wing, wide open.
Butler Yes, milord.

Mint has again drained his glass. The Butler begins to fill his glass again

Amanda Herbert . . .
Butler Yes, miss?
Amanda No-one's come across a diamond ear-ring while they've been cleaning have they?
Butler Not to my knowledge, no, miss . . .
Amanda Oh. Pity.

Mint has drained his glass. The Butler begins to fill his glass

Lady Slingsby-Craddock Herbert . . .
Butler Milady?
Lady Slingsby-Craddock I think we'll have Turkish coffee, this evening . . .
Butler Yes, milady.

Mint has drained his glass. The Butler refills it

Lord Slingsby-Craddock No we bally well won't, Herbert . . . that'll finish me completely.

Butler Yes, milord.

Mint has drained his glass. The Butler refills it

Lady Slingsby-Craddock Oh well, all right . . . Herbert.
Butler Milady?
Lady Slingsby-Craddock One ordinary coffee for his Lordship.
Butler Yes, milady.

Mint has drained his glass. The Butler empties the dregs of the bottle into his glass and stares at it in surprise. Mint takes the bottle from him, tilts it over his glass, hands it back. Nods and smiles to the Butler

The Butler exits

Mint, now very tight, attempts to tackle his steak. He picks up a knife and fork and wrestles with it. The plate, in the struggle which is quite prolonged, slips off the table into his lap and on to the floor. The others look up momentarily. Mint looks nonchalant. They continue eating. Mint slides sideways, as inconspicuously as possible to retrieve the plate. He still clutches his knife and fork. He is forced to start again several times, as someone looks up from their meal. He retrieves the plate successfully. He now goes after the steak which is more difficult. In his search he all but disappears

The Butler enters and removes his plate

The Maid enters with an exotic sweet. She puts it on his place

Mint emerges triumphant with his piece of steak. He slaps it in his exotic sweet. He stares at it in dismay. The Butler disdainfully moves in and removes Mint's sweet. Mint puts his knife and fork in his pocket

Lady Slingsby-Craddock We ought to drink a toast, you know.
Amanda Oh yes . . .
Cecil What a good idea.
Lady Slingsby-Craddock Don't you think so, Edward?
Lord Slingsby-Craddock Toast?
Lady Slingsby-Craddock To Amanda and Cecil.
Amanda Oh, Mummy, no . . .
Lady Slingsby-Craddock Let's drink to Amanda and Cecil.
Amanda Mummy, no, no, no . . .
Lady Slingsby-Craddock (*rising*) Stand up everybody.
Amanda (*twisting herself in embarrassment*) Mummy, no, no, no . . .
Lady Slingsby-Craddock Don't be silly darling . . .
Amanda No, Mummy . . .
Lady Slingsby-Craddock Absent friends then. Let's drink to absent friends . . .
Cecil Good idea, absent friends . . .
Lady Slingsby-Craddock Ready everybody. Edward . . . will you?
Lord Slingsby-Craddock All right then—er . . . um . . . er . . . I . . . er . . . (*He clears his throat*) To—er . . . the . . . er—absent friends.
All Absent friends!

They have all risen. Piano music. They all drink. But Mint, who is finally overcome by the wine, slides gracefully under the table. When the toast is completed and the others sit, Mint has entirely disappeared. The others tackle their fish without noticing his absence

The following directions, as with much of the preceding business, should finally be taken at high speed, just quick enough for the audience to grasp without being slow enough for them to see clearly the mechanics of the thing:

Mint's hand comes from under the table and unobserved removes Lord Slingsby-Craddock's glass

Lord Slingsby-Craddock goes to drink, finds his glass missing and looks round vainly behind him and round the table

Mint returns Lord Slingsby-Craddock's glass by Lady Slingsby-Craddock

Lord Slingsby-Craddock observes his glass by her, glares and rises to fetch it

As Lord Slingsby-Craddock is moving up to Lady Slingsby-Craddock Mint puts a glass on Lord Slingsby-Craddock's place

Lord Slingsby-Craddock returns with his glass from Lady Slingsby-Craddock who looks injured and innocent, and sees the glass now in his place. He pauses for a second

Mint takes Cecil's glass

Lord Slingsby-Craddock returns with the glass he has taken from Lady Slingsby-Craddock

Cecil seeing that his glass has gone, takes Lord Slingsby-Craddock's

Mint puts a glass by Amanda

Lord Slingsby-Craddock returns to his place. He finds his glass missing, looks round exasperated, sees Amanda has two, moves round to her

Mint puts a glass on Lord Slingsby-Craddock's place

Lord Slingsby-Craddock takes Amanda's glass and moves away

Amanda looks after him protestingly. Mint takes Amanda's other glass

Amanda takes Cecil's glass

Lord Slingsby-Craddock, seeing a glass on his place returns with Amanda's

Cecil takes Lord Slingsby-Craddock's

Lord Slingsby-Craddock returns the glass to Amanda

Mint puts a glass by Lady Slingsby-Craddock

Lord Slingsby-Craddock returns to his place, sees his glass is missing and moves up to Lady Slingsby-Craddock

Mint puts a glass on Lord Slingsby-Craddock's place

Lord Slingsby-Craddock takes a glass from Lady Slingsby-Craddock, returns to his place, sees a glass there. Gives up, sits down

Mint puts a glass by Amanda

Lady Slingsby-Craddock, noticing she has a spare glass still, passes it down the table via Amanda to Lord Slingsby-Craddock

Mint puts a glass by Cecil

Amanda passes her two spare glasses, plus Lady Slingsby-Craddock's to Cecil

Cecil pases the three he has received plus his own spare to Lord Slingsby-Craddock

Lord Slingsby-Craddock, adding his own spare glass to them, lines the five spare glasses across the table in front of Mint's place

They all stare at them for a minute. Then at each other. Mint's hand comes up from his own side and adds a bottle

The others look back sharply as they hear it. Then, rising with one accord, they all lean over to Mint's side waiting for him to come up

Mint comes up swiftly so that he is sitting between Amanda and Cecil

The others sit. A long silence. Nobody looks at anybody

Lord Slingsby-Craddock (*finally, raising his glass, quietly*) Absent friends . . .
All (*raising glasses*) Absent friends.

Scene P

Lady Slingsby-Craddock (*suddenly, violently*) Oh, just look at that moon . . .

All the Lights go out. An absurd moon dangles over their heads. They all rise and cluster under it, making moon gazing noises

Whilst this is in progress, the Butler and Maid clear the table, stools, chairs etc.

Amanda Isn't it glorious? It's completely full.
Cecil Absolutely amazing . . .
Lady Slingsby-Craddock Isn't it wonderful, quite wonderful. Oh, I adore the moon, it makes me want to sing . . . (*Trilling*) La—la, la, la, la . . .
Amanda Mummy . . .
Lord Slingsby-Craddock You'll frighten the bally horses in a minute, Val . . .
Lady Slingsby-Craddock (*oblivious*) La, la, la, la . . .
Amanda Do you think there are really people living there?
Cecil What, on the moon? Good heavens no.
Amanda Oh, well I read a book . . .

Cecil No, no . . .
Lady Slingsby-Craddock We'll soon find out. Hulloooo—hullooo—up there——
Amanda Mummy . . .
Lady Slingsby-Craddock All together . . . Hullloooooo . . .
All (*in baying unison*) Hullllooooooo . . . !

The moon turns blue

Amanda Oh . . . Look!
Cecil Oh, I say . . .
Lord Slingsby-Craddock Now look what you've done, Val.
Lady Slingsby-Craddock What a glorious blue. It goes with the curtains. Look everybody it goes with the curtains . . .
Cecil I say, something's going on up there.
Amanda Look!
Lady Slingsby-Craddock Shhhh!

The moon explodes and goes out. Disappointed noises

Amanda Oh dear.
Lady Slingsby-Craddock Never mind.
Cecil Jolly odd that. Jolly odd.
Lady Slingsby-Craddock Lights, somebody!
Lord Slingsby-Craddock Just coming. Find the switch.

The Lights come on. Lord Slingsby-Craddock is by the door, Lady Slingsby-Craddock half-way to it, Cecil behind her. Mint and Amanda in an embrace at the window. They part hastily

Lord Slingsby-Craddock (*covering the silence*) Well—I don't know about anybody else, but I'm going to turn in.
Lady Slingsby-Craddock Yes, what a good idea. I expect you're tired, too, Amanda dear.
Amanda Oh, no, not really, Mummy.
Lady Slingsby-Craddock Oh, but you must be dear. And remember we're going to the gymkhana tomorrow.
Amanda No, honestly, Mummy . . .
Lady Slingsby-Craddock You must be tired, darling . . .
Amanda No, Mummy—really.
Lord Slingsby-Craddock (*terminating the discussion*) *You're tired girl.*
Amanda Good-night everybody.
Cecil I'll see you to your room. (*He moves to the door with her*)
Amanda Oh, my hanky . . . (*She returns momentarily to the window and Mint. Whispering*) Tonight . . .

She gives Mint a sharp glance. Mint gives a rather obvious secretive nod. Cecil's eyes narrow

Good-night, everybody.
Lord Slingsby-Craddock Good-night.
Lady Slingsby-Craddock Good-night.

Cecil Good-night.
Lord Slingsby-Craddock Good-night.
Lady Slingsby-Craddock Good-night.
Amanda Good-night.

Amanda and Cecil exit

Lady Slingsby-Craddock (*to Mint*) Good-night.

Lady Slingsby-Craddock exits

Lord Slingsby-Craddock stands for a long time as if to say something

Lord Slingsby-Craddock Good-night.

Lord Slingsby-Craddock exits

Mint stands smiling

Lady Slingsby-Craddock enters

Lady Slingsby-Craddock (*hurriedly*) Tonight . . .

She blows a kiss, smiles and exits

Mint stands stupefied. He shrugs and goes off after Lord and Lady Slingsby-Craddock

Scene Q

The upper landing. Three passages lead off and meet centre-stage in a T-junction. As a reference for the following business, the passages are labelled; the top two X and Y, and the bottom one Z

This is a going-to-bed sequence. Lady Slingsby-Craddock, Amanda and Cecil all know where they're going, Lord Slingsby-Craddock is looking for an empty bathroom. Mint has lost his bedroom. The background bathroom noises should steadily grow in volume, till the entire plumbing throughout the house is singing in unison

Amanda enters from X carrying a sponge-bag

Lord and Lady Slingsby-Craddock enter from Z

Amanda (*passing Lord and Lady Slingsby-Craddock*) Good-night.
Lady Slingsby-Craddock Good-night.
Lord Slingsby-Craddock Good-night.

Amanda exits Z

Lord and Lady Slingsby-Craddock separate

Lady Slingsby-Craddock goes up to X and exits

Lord Slingsby-Craddock goes up to Y

Cecil enters from Y with his sponge-bag. He passes Lord Slingsby-Craddock

Cecil Good-night.
Lord Slingsby-Craddock Good-night.

Lord Slingsby-Craddock exits Y

Amanda enters from Z without her sponge-bag. She passes Cecil

Amanda Good-night.
Cecil Good-night.

Cecil exits Z

Lady Slingsby-Craddock enters from X. She passes Amanda

Lady Slingsby-Craddock Good-night.
Amanda Good-night.

Amanda exits X

Mint enters from Z. He passes Lady Slingsby-Craddock at the intersection

Lady Slingsby-Craddock Tonight.

Mint smiles and hurries on, to exit X

Lord Slingsby-Craddock enters Y. He carries a loofah

He passes Lady Slingsby-Craddock. She smiles, he grunts

Lady Slingsby-Craddock exits Y

Cecil enters from Z. He passes Lord Slingsby-Craddock at the intersection

Cecil Good-night.
Lord Slingsby-Craddock Good-night.

Lord Slingsby-Craddock exits X

Mint enters from Y. He passes Cecil

Cecil (*coolly*) Good-night.

Mint gives him a cod salute

Cecil glares and exits Y

Amanda enters X passing Mint. She now carries the loofah

Amanda Tonight . . .

A fleeting kiss. They hear someone

Mint exits X

Lady Slingsby-Craddock enters Y. She passes Amanda

Lady Slingsby-Craddock Good-night.
Amanda Good-night.

Amanda exits Y

Lord Slingsby-Craddock enters from X

Lady Slingsby-Craddock exits Z

Cecil enters from Y. He now carries the loofah. He passes Lord Slingsby-Craddock

Cecil Good-night.
Lord Slingsby-Craddock (*sourly*) Good-night.

Mint, who is following close behind Cecil from Y gives Lord Slingsby-Craddock a wave in passing

Lord Slingsby-Craddock exits Y

Lady Slingsby-Craddock enters from Z. She passes first Cecil

Lady Slingsby-Craddock Good-night.
Cecil Good-night.

Cecil exits Z

Then Lady Slingsby-Craddock passes Mint, and blows a kiss. Mint smacks his lips back at her

Mint exits Z

Lady Slingsby-Craddock exits X

Mint enters almost immediately now carrying the loofah. He pauses C, *alone. He seems desperate. He closes his eyes, points a finger, spins round on his toes. Selecting a direction in which to go, he exits Z again*

Amanda and Lord Slingsby-Craddock enter from Y

Simultaneously Lady Slingsby-Craddock enters from X

Cecil followed by Mint enter from Z in time to meet both parties at the intersection

All Good-night.

Cecil exits Y

Amanda and Lady Slingsby-Craddock exit Z

Lord Slingsby-Craddock exits X

Mint is left standing. Suddenly he runs like a maniac to exit X, opens a door, steps inside and slams it behind him. He stands breathing heavily. His eyes closed, a look of relief on his face. Almost at once a knock on the door. Mint jumps. He opens the door

It is the Butler. He silently hands Mint a pair of bedroom slippers and a long white night-gown and night-cap. He bows and withdraws. Mint closes the door

Mint holds the night-gown up and studies it. He then takes off his shoes, throws them in the closet. He puts on the long night-gown over his other clothes. Then the night-cap. He studies himself in the mirror, pulls a few faces, does a little dance. He stretches, yawns, climbs into bed and lies down. Fade Lights

Scene R

A slight silence. A distant clock chimes. An owl hoots

One by one, the Lights come up on the separate bedrooms, revealing the occupants sleeping in their various ways

First Lord and Lady Slingsby-Craddock are revealed. Lord Slingsby-Craddock starts a sort of nocturnal chorus. He snores deeply. After a moment Lady Slingsby-Craddock stirs and starts smacking her lips. Lord Slingsby-Craddock fades out as she fades in. The Lights fade on Lady Slingsby-Craddock. She stops her noises. They come up on Amanda who is lying on her back making pleasurable sighs at short intervals. The Lights on Amanda fade and come up on Cecil who is mumbling and chuckling intermittently in his sleep. The Lights on Cecil fade and come up on Mint who is making a short panting sound

The Lights, presently, reveal Cecil again, who adds his mumbling and chuckling to Mint's panting. Then Amanda is added to the scene. She recommences her sighing. Finally on Lord and Lady Slingsby-Craddock. She first, then he, add their noises to the nocturnal babble

There is a very loud screech of an owl. The noises from them stop abruptly. They all sit bolt upright in bed. Lord Slingsby-Craddock has grabbed a large shotgun from beside him and holds it at the ready. They all relax. They lie back with the exception of Mint who sits for a moment, listening. The clock strikes, again, the half-hour

Mint very softly levers himself out of bed and starts for the door. He hops about and draws in his breath. The floor is cold. He puts on his bedroom slippers. At each step they let out an appalling squeak. Mint registers alarm and tries to counteract it. In vain. He carries on. He opens his door softly. It is dark in the passage. He fumbles in his pocket, finds a box of matches and strikes one. He continues a few paces. The match goes out

Cecil is aroused again. He sits up in bed listening. A few squeaks from Mint. Cecil, suspicions aroused, gets out of bed. He is wearing a night attire, identical to that of Mint. Cecil puts on his slippers and crosses to his door. He opens it. Mint strikes another match. He is now roughly at the intersection. Cecil freezes, listening. Mint's match goes out. More squeaks. Cecil fumbles hastily in his pocket and finds a matchbox. He strikes a match and starts off down the passage till his match goes out. Mint strikes another match. He is now near entrance Z, between Amanda's and Lord and Lady Slingsby-

Craddock's rooms. Cecil strikes another match and moves down to the intersection, heading in the direction of exit X

Mint, seeing his light, hastily extinguishes his own and goes out exit Z, squeaking

Lady Slingsby-Craddock hears this and sits up in bed sharply. She smiles to herself and rises carefully to avoid disturbing her husband. She puts on her slippers and tiptoes to the door, opens it and listens. Cecil strikes another match. He is now up by exit X outside Mint's door. He peers around him till his match goes out. Lady Slingsby-Craddock tiptoes back, collects a box of matches from the bedside. She crosses back to the door, steps out into the passage and strikes a match. She moves towards the intersection

In the next sequence Cecil turns back from exit X and starts to move back towards the intersection. He moves more slowly than Lady Slingsby-Craddock who is moving up towards him and exit X. Lady Slingsby-Craddock's first match goes out. Cecil strikes a match. As soon as it goes out, Lady Slingsby-Craddock strikes a match. She moves up to just before the corner to exit X. The match goes out. The next matches are struck together as Lady Slingsby-Craddock and Cecil are almost nose to nose. A shrill cry of alarm from them both. The matches go out

Lady Slingsby-Craddock goes out exit X in the Black-out

Cecil continues slowly down to the intersection. Lord Slingsby-Craddock has been re-awakened by the shout. He seizes his gun. Noticing Lady Slingsby-Craddock missing he rises, and goes to the door, searching first for matches by the bed, then in his pocket. He opens his door. Cecil strikes a match. Lord Slingsby-Craddock, roused, cocks his gun and tucks it under his arm. Cecil's match goes out. Lord Slingsby-Craddock strikes a match and starts up towards the intersection. His match goes out. Cecil strikes another match. He moves nearer to Lord Slingsby-Craddock. It goes out. Lord Slingsby-Craddock strikes another and Cecil almost simultaneously does the same, revealing that they have somehow passed each other. Lord Slingsby-Craddock is now past the intersection and heading to exit X. Cecil is in the passage to exit Z. Their matches go out

Mint, under cover of darkness, moves in from exit Z to within a few inches of Cecil. We hear the squeak of his bedroom slippers

He and Cecil strike matches simultaneously. Another cry. Black-out. Cecil, in darkness, retreats to the intersection and remains. Mint is in Amanda's room. Lord Slingsby-Craddock, still up by exit X, strikes a match, looks suspiciously in the direction of the noise. His match goes out. Mint strikes a match in Amanda's room close to Amanda. She sits up with a stifled cry. Mint holds up his hand

Amanda (*holding out her arms for him, in a whisper*) Oh . . . Mr Whatnot . . .

They embrace. Mint makes a warning gesture that they must be quiet. He helps her out of bed. They tiptoe to the door

Lady Slingsby-Craddock enters from entrance Y and strikes a match. She moves on towards the intersection

Cecil, still at the intersection, strikes a match. Lord Slingsby-Craddock moving down now from exit X strikes a match. All three matches go out. Now everyone moves to the intersection. Amanda and Mint from Z. Lord Slingsby-Craddock from X. Lady Slingsby-Craddock from Y. They gather round Cecil. Everyone strikes matches simultaneously. Screams from the women, yells from Cecil, a roar of triumph from Lord Slingsby-Craddock. This is all topped by a deafening explosion. A shrill scream from Lady Slingsby-Craddock

Cecil Lights!

Mint and Amanda exit X

The Lights in the hall come on. There is now silence. Lord Slingsby-Craddock stands at one end of the passage still holding his gun. Cecil stands cowering at the other. Between them Lady Slingsby-Craddock is stretched out. Cecil and Lord Slingsby-Craddock regard each other. Lord Slingsby-Craddock clears his throat nervously. They move in cautiously on Lady Slingsby-Craddock

(*In almost a whisper*) I say sir . . .

Lady Slingsby-Craddock stirs, groans. They kneel by her

Lady Slingsby-Craddock My leg . . .
Lord Slingsby-Craddock Val . . . I—er . . . I . . . sorry.
Lady Slingsby-Craddock (*hazily*) Mr . . . Whatnot . . .
Cecil (*from a window*) Look sir . . .
Lord Slingsby-Craddock What?
Cecil It's them. Amanda and Mr . . .
Lady Slingsby-Craddock (*murmuring*) Mr Whatnot . . .
Lord Slingsby-Craddock (*at the window*) What?
Cecil (*pointing*) Look . . .
Lord Slingsby-Craddock Good heavens. It's that bally man Mr—er . . .
Lady Slingsby-Craddock Mr Whatnot . . .
Lord Slingsby-Craddock Mr Whatnot. Get after them, man.

Lord Slingsby-Craddock runs to exit X. Cecil runs to exit Y

Herbert!
Lady Slingsby-Craddock (*abandoned*) Help!
Lord Slingsby-Craddock (*to Cecil*) Wait!

Cecil stops

Bring her . . . I'll get the car.

Lord Slingsby-Craddock exits X

Cecil levers Lady Slingsby-Craddock up and supports her injured side

Lady Slingsby-Craddock (*slightly delirious*) Thank you, Mr Whatnot, you're so kind . . .
Cecil That's quite all right. This way if you can manage . . .

Lady Slingsby-Craddock (*singing as before*) La-la, la, la, la . . .

Cecil and Lady Slingsby-Craddock exit

Scene S

Chase music

Mint and Amanda are running. They reach the car

Mint helps Amanda, still in her long white night-dress and bare-footed, aboard. Mint runs round to the driver's seat. He runs back, cranks the car. He nods to Amanda who presses something. It roars into life

At the other corner of the stage Lord Slingsby-Craddock enters, still with his shotgun and in night attire. He leaps aboard his car. He presses the self-starter. The car starts smoothly. He waves behind him for Cecil and Lady Slingsby-Craddock to follow

They enter, one still supporting the other, and all squeeze into the front seat, Lady Slingsby-Craddock in the middle

Mint has run back to the driver's seat and moves off. A chase sequence:

Mint, concentrating furiously on the road ahead, drives for dear life. Amanda alternates her attention between the road ahead which frightens her and the car behind, which terrifies her. Lord Slingsby-Craddock is also concentrating on his driving though on one occasion he stands up in his seat and fires off a round at the fugitives. Amanda seeing his intention warns Mint and they both duck. Lady Slingsby-Craddock and Cecil, alarmed, pull Lord Slingsby-Craddock back into his seat. He steers the car back on to the road just in time

Mint passes the Pedestrian on his bicycle

They recognize each other and wave. The Pedestrian turns his machine round and pedals up level with Mint. Mint explains his predicament soundlessly, drowned by the engine of the car. The Pedestrian nods, turns his machine round and drops behind. The Pedestrian has parked his bicycle right in the middle of the road in front of Lord Slingsby-Craddock's car. Lord Slingsby-Craddock treads on the brakes. He sounds the horn

Lord Slingsby-Craddock Get out of the way, man!

The Pedestrian indicates he is pumping up his tyres

Cecil Come on then, chappie.
Lord Slingsby-Craddock Hurry, man.

The Pedestrian continues in a leisurely manner. Lord Slingsby-Craddock impatiently jumps from the car and grabs the pump. He works it vigorously, becomes exhausted after a few seconds and waves to Cecil who takes over the task

Amanda looking behind her, now sees no sign of their pursuers. Mint glances round, looks at her and smiles. They whoop silently and embrace. Mint hastily grabs the wheel

Cecil is still pumping. Lord Slingsby-Craddock glances impatiently at his watch. The Pedestrian stands contentedly. He steps forward from time to time to squeeze the tyre, then shakes his head. Cecil finally gives up. He hands the Pedestrian the pump and reels back to the car. Lord Slingsby-Craddock waves the Pedestrian on and returns to the car. They sit impatiently while the Pedestrian mounts his machine. Lord Slingsby-Craddock sounds the horn. The Pedestrian waves and goes to pedal off. Loud hissing sound as his tyre goes down. He shrugs and indicates the tyre and makes to dismount. Lord Slingsby-Craddock threatens him with his gun

The Pedestrian exits fast

Lord Slingsby-Craddock starts the car again. Drives off

Mint is still driving. Amanda is subdued and now looks most miserable. She is huddled up shivering and bedraggled. Mint sees her predicament and stops. He stands up and starts to take off his night-shirt. Amanda registers shock then relief as Mint reveals himself, fully dressed. He wraps his night-shirt round her. He finds a rug. He puts that round her. Finally, he all but wraps himself round her. She starts to sob. Mint holds her unhappily. He looks at the sky and wonders what to do

Lord Slingsby-Craddock has also stopped the car. The three are all leaning on each other, fast asleep. Lord Slingsby-Craddock is snoring, Lady Slingsby-Craddock smacks her lips and Cecil mutters and chuckles to himself

The Lights fade. A clap of thunder. A sharp flash of lightning, a furious downpour

Mint is still holding the sleeping Amanda. In his other hand he holds an umbrella over them. He looks more mournful than ever. The trio in the other car sit bedraggled under a piece of newspaper

Lord and Lady Slingsby-Craddock and Cecil exit in the Black-out

The Lights come up

Birdsong. It is morning. The rain has stopped although there is a rhythmic dripping as the trees drip on the car

Mint is still holding Amanda and the umbrella, though this is now resting on the ground. The couple are asleep. Mint awakes with a start and looks around. He realizes where he is. He looks down at Amanda and kisses her forehead. She groans. Mint tries to get his arm from under her. He does so with difficulty. He gives a silent scream at the pain in his arm. He rubs it and clambers out of the car. He lets down the umbrella. He stands for a moment inhaling. He tries to wake Amanda. She groans. He tries again. She groans, levers herself up and opens her eyes. Mint smiles at her. She groans, closes her eyes again. Mint holds her face in his hands. She groans and clings to him. He strokes her hair and sits her round in the driving seat. He kisses her. She gives a little whimper

Mint attempts to start the car. There is not a sound from the engine. He shrugs and gives up. Amanda groans. Mint gives her his hand. She looks reluctant to get out. He coaxes her. She does so finally. She cries out as her feet come in contact with the wet grass. She sits back in the car. Mint holds out his arms offering to carry her. She looks doubtful. He looks determined. She consents. Mint staggers with her a few paces. He drops her. Amanda looks at him indignantly. Mint rubs his arm and shakes his head, by way of an excuse. Amanda giggles. He takes her hand. They pick their way across what must be a meadow or ploughed field. Amanda stepping gingerly and giggling intermittently

They go off as the Lights fade

As they exit, Lord and Lady Slingsby-Craddock, Cecil and the Tweedy Lady march on in pursuit and exit as rapidly

Scene T

A church. Just before the morning service. A loud, single church bell is ringing

The Vicar, on the end of a bell rope, swings into view, cassock flying

Mint and Amanda enter after a moment. They conduct a silent conversation with the Vicar, obviously trying to persuade him to let them get married

The Vicar, at first, seems reluctant, but a quick exchange of money persuades him. Mint gleefully joins in the bell ringing with the Vicar. Bells ring everywhere

As they die away, Mint hurriedly exits

The Vicar positions Amanda at the top of the aisle

Mint returns with a length of veil and a large flower—possibly a dandelion or something similarly incongruous. He drapes Amanda with the veil and presents her with the flower

The Vicar gives a wave to the organist in the loft. The wedding march strikes up. Mint and Amanda start solemnly down the aisle. Amanda glances over her shoulder, reacts in horror and indicates to Mint who signals to the Vicar to tell the organist to speed things up. He does. They arrive at the altar at a canter. The Vicar, infected by the tempo, holds up his hand. The organist stops abruptly

Vicar Have you the ring?

Mint nods and fumbles in his pocket. A shower of knives and forks cascade over the floor. They hastily gather them up. Mint returns them to his pocket. Produces a ring

Do you—Mr er—er . . .

Amanda Whatnot.

Vicar Do you, Mr Whatnot, take this woman to be your lawfully wedded wife?

Lord Slingsby-Craddock enters at this precise moment from the back of the church. He is followed by the others

Lord Slingsby-Craddock (*roaring*) No! He does not. Don't know the bally fellow from Adam.

He advances down the aisle on Mint. The others, rushing in, collide into the back of him. The gun explodes. Mint clutches his chest. The Vicar swoons. Mint staggers round, does an elaborate mock death. The others stand aghast

He rises, puts his hand inside his jacket and produces a large bent spoon. He smiles, throws it in the air and dashes off

Lady Slingsby-Craddock Stop him!

Tweedy Lady Leave the fellow, Val, leave him.

Lord Slingsby-Craddock (*turning to Amanda*) As for you——

Amanda Daddy . . .

Lady Slingsby-Craddock No, Edward, don't. She was abducted.

Lord Slingsby-Craddock Someone revive that fellow, will you?

Cecil runs forward to the Vicar, leaving the Tweedy Lady to support Lady Slingsby-Craddock

Cecil (*bending over the vicar*) I say, do wake up.

The Vicar groans, Cecil helps him to his feet

Vicar A thunderbolt.

Lord Slingsby-Craddock All right, let's get organized.

He assembles them into a marriage group, Cecil on the Vicar's left, Amanda next to him on the Vicar's right, the Tweedy Lady behind Cecil. He supports Lady Slingsby-Craddock behind Amanda

All right then, carry on, Vicar.

Amanda Oh, Daddy . . .

Lord Slingsby-Craddock Doesn't seem to matter to you *who* you marry, what are you moaning about? It means a lot to me. Where were you, go on from there . . .

Vicar Oh yes er . . . Do you . . . Mr—er Whatnot . . .

Cecil Cecil.

Vicar Take this woman to be your lawful wedded wife?

Cecil Rather.

Vicar Do you——

Amanda Amanda.

Vicar Take this man to be your lawful wedded husband?

Amanda (*sulkily*) Yes—I do . . .

Vicar Would you put the ring on her finger, please . . .

Cecil (*who doesn't have one*) Oh . . . I . . .
Lord Slingsby-Craddock (*snatching one off his own finger, a large signet*) Here.

Cecil puts the ring on Amanda's finger

Vicar I pronounce you man and wife.

Lady Slingsby-Craddock and the Tweedy Lady cheer. The former feebly, the latter lustily. They both blow their noses

Cecil Jolly good show.
Lord Slingsby-Craddock Well go on man, kiss her.

Cecil lifts Amanda's veil and does so, rather half-heartedly

Cecil Hallo.

The Vicar signals to the choir and organist. They strike up the "Eton Boating Song". The bride and groom walk up the aisle. The Tweedy Lady throws confetti. Cecil and Amanda continue up the aisle. The others drop back. Cecil and Amanda turn at the top of the aisle. The Lights are now fading on all but them

Vicar (*from the gloom*) Smile please.

Amanda and Cecil take on fixed wedding photo smiles and remain frozen thus for a few moments. During which: the Lights fade till a solo spot on them is all that remains

The others clear the stage

The "Eton Boating Song" fades

Scene U

Amanda and Cecil step forward

Cecil Well, this is my little flat. Hope you're going to like it. All a bit of a rush this wedding business. Otherwise I'd have tidied up a bit.

He opens the front door. Amanda walks in. Her manner is now listless and dejected

(*Nervously looking round, waiting for her reaction*) Well . . . What do you think?
Amanda (*without conviction*) Gorgeous.
Cecil Do you think so?
Amanda Simply gorgeous.
Cecil Oh good. (*He smiles. He stands looking at her. He takes her shoulders tentatively, then releases them*) Well . . . How about some coffee. Fancy a spot of coffee?
Amanda No, thank you.

Cecil No, perhaps it is a bit late. Well . . . time for—er . . . bed . . . I suppose.

The bed enters. Strains of the "Eton Boating Song"

Amanda Yes.
Cecil (*consulting his watch*) My word yes, it's time for bed. Good heavens above, yes. Definitely bedtime. I'll show you your room, shall I?
Amanda (*deflated*) Yes.

Cecil leads the way

Cecil This way. Mind your head there. Here we are. Nothing luxurious. Quite cosy though.

Amanda gets into bed. She slides down. A pair of feet appear at the bottom of the bed as she pulls the counterpane around her

I'll be downstairs if you—er . . . want anything. Just bang on the floor.
Amanda Good-night.

Cecil takes her shoulders for a moment, then releases her

Cecil Yes. Just bang—on—the—floor. 'Night.
Amanda 'Night.

Cecil pats her feet and exits

Amanda snuggles down the bed. A second pair of feet, her own, appear, either side of the first pair. She frowns and gapes

(*Ecstatic*) Oh, Mr Whatnot!!

Mint brings an arm out from under her. The other arm switches off the light. Hasty Black-out

CURTAIN

FURNITURE AND PROPERTY LIST

ACT I

Scene A

Mint's house

On stage: Chair

Personal: **Mint:** Door key
Mint: Small black bag, newspaper

Scene B

The drawing-room at the Grange

On stage: Revolving piano stool

Personal: **Lord** and **Lady Slingsby-Craddock:** large sunhats
Lord Slingsby-Craddock: shooting stick
Amanda: large sunhat
Cecil: large sunhat
Tweedy Lady: large sunhat

Scene C

Mint's house. The Grange

On stage: Chairs

Scene D

Outside Mint's house

On stage: Starting handle

Off stage: Bicycle handlebars **(Pedestrian)**

Personal: **Pedestrian:** Spanner

Scene E

The grounds of the Grange

Off stage: Motormower handlebars **(Gardener)**
Bicycle handlebars **(Pedestrian)**

Personal: **Mint:** Goggles and hat

SCENE F

The Grange

No props required

SCENE G

The Grange

Off stage: Deckchair **(Amanda)**
Cocktail **(Amanda)**
Box of chocolates **(Cecil)**

SCENE H

The Grange

Personal: **Mint:** Tuning fork

SCENE I

The grounds of the Grange

No props required

SCENE J

The tennis court

Personal: **Amanda:** Racket
Cecil: Racket
Lady Slingsby-Craddock: Racket
Tweedy Lady: Racket

SCENE K

The grounds of the Grange

Off stage: Small table *On it:* plates of sandwiches, rolls, side plates **(Lady Slingsby-Craddock)**
Cakestand and chair **(Cecil)**
2 chairs **(Amanda)**
2 chairs **(Tweedy Lady)**

Personal: **Mint:** White handkerchief

SCENE L

Mint's bedroom at the Grange

On stage: Bed

ACT II

Scene M

Bedrooms at the Grange

On stage: Dinner jacket and tie

Personal: **Mint:** Shoe brush
Mint: Watch
Lady Slingsby-Craddock: Jewellery

Scene N

The dining-room at the Grange

Off stage: Long oblong table. *On it:* large white tablecloth, cutlery, five wineglasses, two candelabras **(Butler** and **Maid)**
Chair **(Butler)**
Chair **(Maid)**
Bench **(Butler)**
Bench **(Maid)**
Large menu **(Butler)**
Rose **(Maid)**
Large bottle of wine **(Butler)**
Gong **(Butler** and **Maid)**

Scene O

The dining-room at the Grange

Off stage: Trolley. *On it:* soup **(Maid** and **Butler)**
Fish **(Maid)**
Steak **(Maid)**
Wine **(Butler)**
Exotic sweet **(Maid)**

Scene P

The dining-room

Off stage: Moon

Scene Q

The upper landing

On stage: Bed

Off stage: Sponge bag **(Amanda)**
Sponge bag **(Cecil)**
Loofah **(Lord Slingsby-Craddock)**
Nightgown, nightcap and slippers **(Butler)**

Scene R

Bedrooms and landing

On stage: Shotgun
Slippers
Box of matches

Personal: **Mint:** Box of matches
Cecil: Box of matches
Lord Slingsby-Craddock: Box of matches

Scene S

A road

On stage: Umbrella

Off stage: Bicycle handlebars **(Pedestrian)**

Personal: **Lord Slingsby-Craddock:** Shotgun, watch
Pedestrian: Bicycle pump

Scene T

A church

On stage: Bell ropes

Off stage: Length of veil **(Mint)**
Large flower **(Mint)**

Personal: **Mint:** Money, knives and forks, ring, bent spoon
Lord Slingsby-Craddock: Ring
The Tweedy Lady: Confetti, handkerchief
Lady Slingsby-Craddock: handkerchief

Scene U

Cecil's flat

On stage: Bed. *On it:* counterpane

LIGHTING PLOT

ACT I

To open: Light on **Mint**'s house

Cue 1 **Mint** sits, reading the newspaper (Page 1)
Lights cross-fade to drawing room

Cue 2 **Lord Slingsby-Craddock:** "Bally thing's brand new." (Page 3)
Bring up lights on **Mint***'s house*

Cue 3 **Mint** stands bemused (Page 4)
Fade lights on **Mint**

Cue 4 **Lord Slingsby-Craddock** and the **Tweedy Lady** go out (Page 4)
Lights cross-fade to **Mint***'s house*

Cue 5 **Pedestrian** overtakes **Mint** and waves (Page 5)
Lights cross-fade to **Amanda** *and* **Cecil** *in the grounds*

Cue 6 **Cecil:** "Hallo ducks." (Page 5)
Lights cross-fade to **Mint**

Cue 7 **Mint** raises his hat in apology (Page 5)
Lights cross-fade to **Amanda** *and* **Cecil**

Cue 8 **Cecil:** "Quack." (Page 6)
Lights cross-fade to **Mint**

Cue 9 **Mint** inhales the air (Page 6)
Lights cross-fade to **Amanda** *and* **Cecil**

Cue 10 **Amanda** sighs deeply (Page 6)
Lights cross-fade to **Mint**

Cue 11 **Lord Slingsby-Craddock**, **Cecil** and **Mint** make war noises (Page 22)
Lights change to dream-like colour

Cue 12 **Tweedy Lady:** "Good luck." (Page 23)
Spot on Cecil

Cue 13 **Amanda** and **Cecil** embrace (Page 23)
Fade spot

Cue 14 **Mint** and **Amanda** step out on to a balcony (Page 24)
Spot on **Mint** *and* **Amanda**

Cue 15 **Mint** and **Amanda** kiss (Page 24)
Fade spot, bring up normal garden lighting

Cue 16 **Lord Slingsby-Craddock:** "Follow me." (Page 26)
Cross-fade to **Mint***'s bedroom*

Cue 17 **Mint** turns off the light (Page 26)
Black-out

ACT II

To open: Light on **Mint**'s bedroom

Cue 18 **Mint** starts to polish his shoes (Page 27)
Lights come up on **Cecil***'s room*

Cue 19 **Cecil** completes his chorus (Page 27)
Lights come up on **Lady Slingsby-Craddock***'s room*

Cue 20 **Lady Slingsby-Craddock** hums "Frère Jacques." (Page 27)
Lights come up on **Amanda***'s room*

Cue 21 **Amanda** and **Lady Slingsby-Craddock** draw their curtains (Page 27)
Black-out in **Amanda** *and* **Lady Slingsby-Craddock***'s rooms*

Cue 22 **Cecil** draws his curtains (Page 27)
Fade lights on **Cecil***'s room*

Cue 23 **Amanda** and **Mint** kiss (Page 29)
Lights change

Cue 24 **Mint** and **Amanda** are at the opera (Page 29)
Spot on the **Maid**

Cue 25 **Mint** and **Amanda** applaud mildly (Page 29)
Cut spot

Cue 26 **Butler** sounds the gong (Page 29)
Return to general lighting

Cue 27 **Lady Slingsby-Craddock:** "Oh, just look at the moon . . ." (Page 34)
Snap off lights, light on moon

Cue 28 **All:** "Hulloooo." (Page 35)
Moon turns blue

Cue 29 **Lady Slingsby-Craddock:** "Shhh!" (Page 35)
Moon explodes and goes out

Cue 30 **Lord Slingsby-Craddock:** "Find the switch." (Page 35)
Snap up lights

Cue 31 **Mint** climbs into bed and lies down (Page 39)
Fade Lights

Cue 32 An howl hoots (Page 39)
Bring up Lights on **Lord** *and* **Lady Slingsby-Craddock**

Cue 33 After a few moments (Page 39)
Cross-fade to **Amanda**

Cue 34 After a few moments (Page 39)
Cross-fade to **Cecil**

Cue 35 After a few moments (Page 39)
Cross-fade to **Mint**

Cue 36 After a few moments (Page 39)
Bring up Lights on **Cecil**, *then* **Amanda**, *then* **Lord** *and* **Lady Slingsby-Craddock**

Cue 37 **Mint** enters the passage (Page 39)
Dim lighting

Cue 38 **Lady Slingsby-Craddock** and **Cecil**'s matches go out (Page 40)
Black-out

Cue 39 **Lady Slingsby-Craddock** exits (Page 40)
Bring up dim lighting

Cue 40 **Lord Slingsby-Craddock** and **Cecil**'s matches go out (Page 40)
Black-out

Cue 41 **Mint** and **Cecil** strike matches (Page 40)
Bring up dim lighting

Cue 42 A cry (Page 40)
Black-out

Cue 43 **Lord Slingsby-Craddock** and others strike matches (Page 40)
Bring up dim lighting as text

Cue 44 **Cecil:** "Lights!" (Page 41)
Bring up Lights

Cue 45 **Cecil** chuckles to himself (Page 43)
Fade Light to Black-out

Cue 46 When ready (Page 43)
Bring up Lights

Cue 47 **Amanda** and **Mint** go off (Page 44)
Fade Lights

Cue 48 When ready (Page 44)
Bring up Lights on church

Cue 49 **Cecil** and **Amanda** walk up the aisle (Page 46)
Lights fade on all but them

Cue 50 **Amanda** and **Cecil** remain frozen (Page 46)
Fade to spot on them

Cue 51 **Amanda** and **Cecil** step forward (Page 46)
Light on **Cecil***'s flat*

Cue 52 **Mint** switches off the light (Page 47)
Black-out

EFFECTS PLOT

ACT I

Cue 1 To open SCENE A (Page 1)
Introductory music

Cue 2 **Mint** enters and stands for a moment (Page 1)
Voice over

Cue 3 **Mint** moves forward (Page 1)
Sequence: keys, **Mint** *opens and closes the door, fills kettle, lights gas, cat purrs, radio plays foreign programme, then piano music*

Cue 4 Lights fade (Page 1)
Music changes

Cue 5 **Cecil** strikes a chord (Page 2)
Chord

Cue 6 **Cecil** plays a chord and a flurry of notes (Page 2)
Chord and flurry of notes

Cue 7 **Cecil:** "Listen to it." (Page 2)
Sequence: treble note, middle note, bass note

Cue 8 **Lady Slingsby-Craddock** opens the telephone book (Page 3)
Boing

Cue 9 **Lady Slingsby-Craddock:** ". . . two—three." (Page 3)
Lord Slingsby-Craddock *dials,* **Mint***'s telephone rings*

Cue 10 **Mint** is reading the newspaper, then answers the telephone (Page 3)
Sequence: music on radio, cut telephone, cut music, kettle whistles, saucepans clatter, phone slams

Cue 11 **Lord Slingsby-Craddock:** "Good dog." (Page 4)
Dog approaches

Cue 12 **Mint** goes out through the front door (Page 4)
Sequence: door slams, crank, crank, splutter, crank, splutter, crank, splutter, horn, crank, engine fires, revs, drives away

Cue 13 **Mint** narrowly misses someone (Page 5)
Skid, horn

Cue 14 **Cecil** and **Amanda** walk in the grounds (Page 5)
Birdsong (continuous), ducks

Cue 15 **Mint** wings something (Page 5)
Skid, crash, skid

Cue 16 **Mint** arrives in the grounds of Craddock Grange (Page 6)
Car stops suddenly with a jolt

Cue 17 **Cecil:** "... I—get—it—and——" (Page 6)
Splash, quack

Cue 18 **Mint** appears to be alone (Page 6)
Motormower

Cue 19 **Lord Slingsby-Craddock:** "... come back here!" (Page 6)
Dog barks and growls in the distance

Cue 20 **Mint** pulls the front door bell (Page 7)
Sequence: doorbell, unfasten door, close door, fade birdsong, doors open and close, footsteps echo, doorbell, doors open and close, door slams, doors open and close, door slams

Cue 21 **Mint** plays a note and three chords (Page 8)
Note, three chords

Cue 22 **Mint** begins to strike a note continuously, then a discord (Page 8)
Notes end with discord

Cue 23 **Mint** treads on the keyboard (Page 8)
Discord

Cue 24 **Mint** sits at the piano (Page 8)
Sweeping chords and trills, "Chopsticks", passionate love songs, funeral march

Cue 25 **Mint** twangs his tuning fork (Page 9)
Twang

Cue 26 **Cecil:** "Is it tuned?" (Page 9)
Sequence: note, note, two notes played simultaneously twice, three notes three times, four bass notes

Cue 27 **Cecil** starts to play (Page 9)
"Für Elise" with discordant notes, becoming shriller and ending with a heavy chord

Cue 28 They all close their eyes (Page 10)
Sequence: "Moonlight Sonata", "Twelfth Street Rag", "Moonlight Sonata", "Twelfth Street Rag", slam of piano lid

Cue 29 **Lord Slingsby-Craddock** enters the garden (Page 11)
Birdsong (continuous)

Cue 30 He whistles his dog (Page 11)
Sequence: dog arrives, recedes, smashing glass

Cue 31 **Mint** whistles to himself (Page 12)
Dog arrives, barks, grapples, growls, recedes

Cue 32 **Cecil** cranks up the net (Page 13)
Squeak of net

Cue 33 **Cecil** hits a ball over the net (Page 13)
Volley 1

Cue 34 The knock-up starts in earnest (Page 13)
Volley 2

Cue 35 **Cecil** serves to **Amanda** (Page 14)
Volley 3

Cue 36 **Cecil** serves again, slower (Page 14)
Volley 4

Cue 37 **Cecil** serves to **Amanda** (Page 15)
Volley 5

Cue 38 **Cecil** serves to **Mint** (Page 16)
Volley 6

Cue 39 **Cecil** serves to **Amanda** (Page 16)
Volley 7

Cue 40 **Cecil** serves to **Mint** (Page 16)
Volley 8

Cue 41 **Cecil** serves to **Mint** (Page 16)
Volley 9

Cue 42 **Cecil** serves to **Amanda** (Page 17)
Volley 10

Cue 43 **Cecil** serves to **Mint** (Page 17)
Volley 11

Cue 44 **Cecil** serves to **Amanda** (Page 17)
Volley 12

Cue 45 **Cecil** serves to **Mint** (Page 17)
Volley 13

Cue 46 **Lady Slingsby-Craddock** enters (Page 18)
Wind (continuous)

Cue 47 **Mint:** "... ber—doing ..." (Page 22)
Sequence: battle noises, whistle, explosion, machine gun, machine gun, explosion, 1940s romantic music, explosions, machine gun, drumming, explosions, cheering, "Land of Hope and Glory"

Cue 48 Balletic sequence (Page 25)
Sequence: music, crash, waltz music. Fade wind

Cue 49 **Mint** bounces on the bed (Page 26)
Bounce

Cue 50 As **Mint** goes to sleep (Page 26)
Piano music

ACT II

Cue 51 To open Scene M (Page 27)
Music. Fade when ready

Cue 52 **Mint** opens the closet door (Page 27)
Door opens and closes

Cue 53 To open Scene N (Page 28)
Sequence: bell chimes, waltz music, Emperor Waltz, Spanish dance, Wagnerian duet, seagulls and sea noises, gong

Cue 54 They have all risen (Page 33)
Piano music (continuous)

Cue 55 **Lady Slingsby-Craddock:** "Oh, just look at the moon." (Page 34)
Moon appears

Cue 56 **Lady Slingsby-Craddock:** "Shhhh!" (Page 35)
Moon explodes

Cue 57 To open SCENE Q (Page 36)
Plumbing (continuous)

Cue 58 **Lord Slingsby-Craddock** exits (Page 38)
Fade plumbing

Cue 59 **Mint** runs to exit X (Page 38)
Sequence: door opens and closes, knock on door, door opens and closes

Cue 60 After a slight silence (Page 39)
Clock chimes, owl hoots

Cue 61 Lights come up on **Lord** and **Lady Slingsby-Craddock** (Page 39)
Owl screeches loudly

Cue 62 **Mint** sits for a moment, listening (Page 39)
Clock chimes the half-hour

Cue 63 As **Mint** walks (Page 39)
Squeak of slippers

Cue 64 **Cecil** opens the door (Page 39)
Door opens and closes

Cue 65 **Lord Slingsby-Craddock** roars triumphantly (Page 41)
Explosion

Cue 66 To open SCENE S (Page 42)
Chase music (continuous)

Cue 67 **Mint** runs to car (Page 42)
Chase sequence: **Mint**'*s car cranks and starts,* **Lord Slingsby-Craddock**'*s car starts, gunshot,* **Mint** *skids,* **Lord Slingsby-Craddock** *skids, horn, car stops, horn, tyre hisses, car starts and drives off,* **Mint** *stops,* **Lord Slingsby-Craddock** *stops*

Cue 68 The Lights fade (Page 43)
Thunder, pouring rain

Cue 69 Lights come up (Page 43)
Birdsong, dripping rain

Cue 70 **Mint** tries to start the car (Page 44)
Car starting noises

Cue 71 They pick their way across a meadow or ploughed field (Page 44)
Piano music

Cue 72 To open SCENE T (Page 44)
Loud single church bell

Cue 73 **Mint** joins in the bell ringing (Page 44)
Bells ring everywhere

Cue 74 **The Vicar** gives a wave to the organist (Page 44)
"Wedding March" begins

Cue 75 They collide into **Lord Slingsby-Craddock** (Page 45)
Gun explodes

Cue 76 **The Vicar** signals to the choir and the organist (Page 46)
"Eton Boating Song"

Cue 77 The others clear the stage (Page 46)
Fade "Eton Boating Song"

Cue 78 The bed enters (Page 47)
"Eton Boating Song"

MADE AND PRINTED IN GREAT BRITAIN BY
LATIMER TREND & COMPANY LTD PLYMOUTH

MADE IN ENGLAND